TRANSNATIONALS
& the Third World

TRANSLATED BY DAVID BUXTON

Transnationals & the Third World

THE STRUGGLE FOR CULTURE

Armand Mattelart

Bergin & Garvey Publishers, Inc.
Massachusetts

Library of Congress Cataloging in Publication Data
Mattelart, Armand.
  Transnationals and the Third World.

  Bibliography: p.
  Includes index.
  1. Underdeveloped areas—International business
enterprises—Social aspects. 2. Cultural diffusion.
I. Title.
HD2755.5.M382 1983   338.8'881724   83-2693
ISBN 0-89789-030-2

First published in 1983 by
Bergin & Garvey Publishers, Inc.
670 Amherst Road
South Hadley, Massachusetts 01075

6789   98765432

Printed in the United States of America

Contents

Acknowledgments

The subject of the following study is the sociocultural impact of transnational firms on developing countries. The United Nations, through the Center on Transnational Corporations, commissioned two separate reports on the subject. According to the terms of the agreement, one was to analyze the "positive impact of transnational firms"; and the other, my responsibility, was to focus on the "negative impact." Moreover, the two reports were to allow the foundations to be laid for policies within the framework of *self-reliance*.

I would like to thank the United Nations, which enabled me to carry out this study and authorized me to publish it independently. It goes without saying that the opinions and judgments expressed throughout this book are solely my responsibility. I am also grateful to all those groups and individuals the world over who helped my research by making available often unpublished reports and documents and by taking the time to reply to some of the numerous questions raised by such a study. On a more personal note, I am indebted to David Buxton, who patiently translated this study from the original French.

Armand Mattelart
Paris

War does not belong to the domain of art and science. . . . It is a conflict of big interests settled in blood. . . . It would be better to compare it to commerce, which is also a conflict of interest and human activity.

Karl von Clausewitz, 1832

1

Memorandum for an Analysis of the Cultural Impact of Transnational Firms

It is difficult to deal with the "positive impact" and the "negative impact" of transnational firms in strictly parallel fashion. It is difficult or even impossible to tackle this question by drawing up debit and credit columns in order to draw conclusions from an overall positive or negative balance sheet. If one proceeds in this way, one runs the risk of having to debate the site and the role occupied by transnational firms in developing countries on a terrain defined by the firms themselves. This amounts to the admission that transnational firms are natural elements rather than highly specific historical forms. The result of such a confinement runs the risk of limiting the response or retort to the transnational firm to a narrow and partial perspective that envisages policies for countering the negative effects of transnational firms exclusively in terms of compensation, human cost, safety barriers, and so forth, as if it were enough to limit or at best repair the consequences of an inescapable process. For the peoples and social groups subjected to this inescapability, there would therefore be no chance in this perspective of breaking away from a dynamic situated outside them. This same perspective would lead one to accept the possibility of dealing with the cultural dimension of development without questioning the notion of development as a cultural form. We know that more and more countries and groups of often extremely different political persuasions as much at the

1

center as the periphery are disputing the axiological character of the very notion of development. In doing this they are only exposing the tautological nature of a good many assertions of transnational firms, "These firms help traditional societies progress and modernize because they are factors of modernization" or "In developing themselves, these firms help backward countries develop themselves." As we are beginning to find out, these assertions are founded on the idea that development, progress, and modernity are neutral concepts, universally acceptable.

This is the central issue. To avoid confining the debate on the sociocultural impact of transnational corporations to a moral trial, limited to separating the wheat from the chaff, the good from the bad, a detour will have to be made. One must start by questioning the conceptual apparatus allowing transnational firms to reproduce the conditions of their survival and legitimacy and to judge or even criticize their actions themselves in order to put right mistakes and excesses without questioning an instant their own nature and function. As everyone knows, it is totally impossible to request transnational firms and the apparatus responsible for naturalizing them through doctrines, analyses, and practices, to scuttle themselves. Another conceptual referent must be called on to get away from this transnational centralism. This appears to be a necessary condition for progressively leading the discussion into the wider field of an examination of an overall model of development with its notions of progress, modernity, culture, and humankind and their fulfillment. This premise and methodological option has repercussions as much on the way of dealing with the evidence as on the type of evidence to select in order to arrive at a policy analysis.

A set of problems emerges when one tries to sketch out a suitable conceptual referent by clarifying the meaning of the sequence and the components expressed in this report's general subject, "the sociocultural impact of transnational firms." This subject raises many questions: What are the implications of the transnational firm as agent? How is this role of agent to be understood? What signification must be given to the term *impact*?

The response to these questions can only be progressive. We have formulated these questions straightaway to try and define the field of operations of this study but above all to lay down the foundations of a thesis that will gradually emerge throughout our analysis.

Transnational Firms as Agents

I will not mention here the problems of isolating the impact (I will come back to the meaning of this word) of transnational firms in relation to other sources of influence (for example, the national education apparatus in relation to commercial television, necessarily linked to the transnational model). Our initial question is this: Does transnational power start and finish with transnational firms? Can one, for example, legitimately speak of the sociocultural impact of one or of several transnational electronic and aerospace firms on the education system of a specific country without linking this or these firms to other agents whose activities, although international, cannot be itemized in the catalogs of transnational firms? Very often these other agents, of one sort or another, are as important in producing an effect at a national level as a transnational firm. Without their logistic backing, transnational firms would not be able to exercise their power. The importance and the nature of these logistic supports and agents can obviously vary between different industrial branches and sectors, and their action can be either sporadic or permanent. Two examples serve to illustrate: the exportation of population policy models and communication policy models. Let us go into more detail on two paradigmatic cases.

Birth Control as Policy

The story, still in the news, of the introduction of contraceptive products and devices in developing countries indicates how close alliances, explicit or implicit, concerted or not, natural or programed, are formed between educational foundations, university research centers, and American pharmaceutical laboratories.[1] The task of creating a use for the contraceptive product and the legitimization of this use are the essential phases in the preparation of markets. Moreover, it is a market that remains considerable, as *Business Week* of 30 April 1979 noted, "The contraceptive market is $3 billion worldwide and overpopulation in countries such as India has spurred new birth control research." How can one ignore the role played in the expansion of transnational pharmaceutical markets by scientific investigations of the AUK type (attitude, use, knowledge), carried out by demographers and sociologists from U.S. universities under the sponsorship of educational foundations, in Asia and Latin America, in order to determine peoples' attitudes to the eventual introduction of the pill or the intrauterine device (IUD), the knowledge they might have of contraceptive methods and the use already made of them? These sociologists have never made a secret of the links that, under scientific cover, they were fitted into. "The principal function of these investigations," wrote a Cornell university sociologist working for the Population Council," is similar to any market study: showing that a demand for the goods and services exists, in this case, a demand for birth control. . . . These studies represent, moreover, a way of beginning an action without attracting controversy. As well as supplying information useful for eventual future programs, the research itself stimulates the interest of the people directly or indirectly implicated and can accelerate the whole process of forming policies."[2]

How can the sociocultural impact of these combined practices be ignored? In a document prepared for a seminar on population policy held at Medellín, Colombia, in the 1960s, a Chicago University sociologist who had become the promoter of a very specific type of population policy, expressed himself as follows:

> The sociologist's affirmation of the necessity of treating people from lower social strata in a mass fashion can appear embarrassing for medical professionals and social workers who bear the brunt of the responsibility in the family planning adoption process. In these two domains, it is an old tradition to treat each person individually. The doctor treats his patients one by one and the social worker proudly considers each case individually so as to give adequate advice. Unfortunately, this doctor-patient, counselor-client perspective is dearer, slower, and requires more human potential than any other imaginable perspective for promoting the adoption of family planning throughout a country. In other words, if doctors launch a family planning program with the same philosophy which inspires them in their professional practice, there will be comparatively little progress made; any progress will be extremely localized, whereas important nuclei of the population will be left aside, leading to a very high per capita price. On the contrary, people must be influenced in mass fashion, as long as it is possible.[3]

How can the adhesion of the masses be rapidly and efficiently promoted? It appears that industrial civilization's modern technique of advertising gives free reign to all sorts of hopes and desires. "Family planning literature should make use of beauty and sex appeal," suggests an Indonesian promotion manual. According to the Chicago sociologist just quoted:

> One can "legitimise" family planning through the publication of the signature of famous, credit-worthy and powerful personalities. Mass means can be used efficiently if information is spread as to the fact that doctors, churchmen, cinema actresses, powerful businessmen, legislators, scientists etc. approve of family planning. Similarly, information on contraceptive use in other countries (for example Spain, Italy, France and other catholic countries) will facilitate approval and acceptance. When planning has been

largely implanted, it is a good idea to foster friendship between birth control practitioners by organising parties for patients, or a Christmas party inviting patients to amuse and refresh themselves as well as chat.[4]

This is one example of the impossibility of grasping the action of a transnational firm in terms of a metaphysical or self-contained absolute.

Promotion of Domestic Satellites

The second example concerns the transfer of new communications technology, or, to be more precise, regional satellites, a domain all the more interesting in that it promises to undergo very rapid expansion during this decade. This example relates the various manouvres by transnational electronic firms, educational foundations, and American university centers, which South American countries had to face between 1967 and 1972.[5] In June 1967 Stanford University published the ASCEND report (Advanced System for Communications and Education in National Development). This report proposed to developing countries "incapable of coming up with a sufficient number of qualified teachers in response to the education demands of their growing populations" the solution of a national satellite telecommunications system. To begin with, it could come to the aid of current and future teachers; a central body would establish a program of courses by the best educators in the country and furnish it to the whole school population, both teachers and students; in the last stage, when teachers would be more experienced, the system's educators would prepare broadcasts aimed at enriching the activity of local teachers, allowing them to dedicate more time to their students. On top of this, at the national communications level, satellite technology would provide underdeveloped countries with high quality communications for business and government, point-to-point communication with inacessible regions, a national data transmission, a facsimile and telegram network, as well as the retransmission of television programs.

The ASCEND report, put out by an American university—on the fringe, therefore, of the transnational network—has, however, been decisive for the establishing of the necessary consensus between the partners on the basis of the credibility of its university label. "Everything takes place," writes a Brazilian researcher, "as if Stanford University were the nerve center where the promotion of tele-education satellites radiates forth to all continents, giving this promotion a scientific status and cultural credentials that viability studies from the laboratories of firms directly concerned in the manufacture could not pretend to." The same Brazilian researcher goes on to question this scientific status.

> What strikes the reader of this report is that it has none of the quality of a university work, if one understands by this the discussion of the theoretical foundations of a line of reasoning and the effort of analyzing and understanding a given problem. The ASCEND report is rather a viability study whose principal ambition is to sell a specific technology. However, it could not be said that it hides its intentions; "Our aim is to show what must be done tomorrow with today's technology so that every nation can incorporate it in its national development plan," write the authors on the first page of the introduction. Or again, "Our hardest task is to persuade people, directly influencing their countries' development plans, to fit into them the concepts that, like ASCEND, are used by modern technology."[6]

In April 1969 on the initiative of a group made up of representatives of American firms like COMSAT (Communications Satellite Corporation), Hughes Aircraft, General Electric; educational foundations; and various American universities, a first meeting was held in Santiago, Chile. Various representatives of Latin American universities were also invited. The result was the creation at Bogota of a body named CAVISAT (Centro Audiovisual Internacional via Satellite), financed by COMSAT and various American industrial corporations, to carry out viability studies, prospective research, opinion polls, and analyses of the potential market. At this same meeting, ten North American universities and ten Latin-American universities, most of whom already had links with American educational foundations, were given the task of preparing programs. The attempt to sell this regional satellite system installation model to Spanish-speaking South America was countered by certain governments, who, at the time, already saw the danger in this project to their right to cultural and educational self-determination. Refusal become irremediable when the directors of CAVISAT expressed their intention to go over the top of this opposition and carry out the project with or without Latin American acceptance. Their hope of doing so alone was based on three premises: the right to free use of broadcast frequencies, the possibility of conferring North American academic degrees on Latin American students and extending recognition to their studies. It was only several years later, that the natural legitimacy of the free use of the broadcast frequencies was to be challenged by the nonaligned movement at UNESCO and other international bodies.

Brazil, which had not participated at the meeting mentioned above, was to determinedly embark on the preparation phase for the installation of a tele-education satellite system, which was only to be interrupted in 1977–78 on the official pretext of the expense of buying a satellite. The time that had passed meanwhile had allowed the Brazilians to see how the arrival of new communications technologies in the near future would reinforce the chain of cultural dependence. Engineers from the Brazilian Institute of Space Research (INPE) were sent to Valley Forge, headquarters of the Space Division of General Electric, to be briefed on the systemic approach called *Systems Engineering Management* (applied science dealing with planning, development, construction, and systems evaluation). The importation of technology was accompanied by the acquisition of a pre-prepared planning method, which in turn forced the Brazilians to create an organization in accordance with the norms of American aerospace firms. The observations of a Brazilian member of this project are revealing. "The Institute of Space Research is an American institution conceived in NASA's image. To appreciate this, a simple stroll to the headquarters at São José dos Campos, is far more instructive than any analysis. The Californian Space Center model has been interiorized to such an extent that it is perceptible at every level, from specialist jargon down to clothes. At the Institute, like at NASA, dark trousers and light-coloured, short-sleeved shirts with matching tie are worn."[7]

A New Cultural Prospector

This last example, in particular, shows us that the actions of transnational firms cannot be understood without reflecting on the genealogy of these firms in their country of origin. It is difficult, therefore, to understand the way in which an American transnational satellite manufacturer operates, without taking into account the fine links woven, with ups and downs, since the Second World War in the United States between the private and public sectors, the civil and military sectors, the university and the state, and the university and industry. The network of alliances and interests connecting the American aerospace electronic industry, sectors of the armed forces, universities and research institutes, and private foundations are the fruit of a historical evolution that cannot easily be set aside.[8] The entire history of modern technology is contained in this matrix—the new communications systems are an example par excellence. This is the case even if in every nation of the 'center,' the relationship between the private and the public or the military is in the course of being redefined.

Day after day the impression is confirmed that the original matrix of the new technologies of communication is far from having disappeared from the political horizon. As recently as March 1982, the *Financial Times* and with it all the transnational business magazines reported that executives of the seventeen major American semiconductor and computer companies along with trade and Pentagon officials had met in Orlando, Florida, to discuss joining forces to combat the soaring costs of research and to create a more united front against Japanese competition. (For certain microprocessors, Japanese firms, supported in their research efforts by their government, hold 70 percent of the world market.) The conference was called by Control Data Corporation. One possibility was for a nonprofit research company to be founded by the participants, who could then tap the results to develop their own products. Even though American electronics firms have sometimes created joint ventures to develop certain products, such a level of cooperation would constitute a veritable revolution in an industry based on the principles of competition and free enterprise. Observers feel that such coordination is so vital to American interests that this initiative is unlikely to be blocked by antitrust laws, less and less applied.

The following question will emerge again and again, Where does the public leave off and the private begin? The question of the links of transnational firms with the state apparatus and the overall body of institutions in their mother country is now central. The first two examples lead us to suspect that the structure of transnational power cannot be reduced to the sum of transnational firms. The transnational firms are a part of an overall system in which they have admittedly the role of central units in a capital expansion model. As the basic organizational form of a world scale production process, they are in this sense the foundation of a cultural, political, and economic system. Their network of natural connections does not come from a conspiratorial strategy but from a logic of development and the reproduction of the conditions of this development. There is nothing strange, consequently, when there exist scientific ventures whose premises coincide with this logic.

It is the sphere of influence of these alliances and connections that must be scrutinized more. Presently the monetarist orientation of *Reaganomics*, which legitimizes private investment as the principal actor of development, signifies without any doubt a redistribution of the roles of other agents (without making them disappear altogether). Transnational firms are increasingly combining functions. The recognition of the marketplace as the principal site in this model of development tends to propel the transnational forward to the rank of educator, researcher, and social and cultural canvasser.[9] In these strategies whereby the market is promoted to the role of regulator of social rivalries and inequalities, private investors and lenders are tending to take over from the cohort of organisms born under the aegis of international "welfare" or aid projects in the 1960s. "The relationship between multinational corporations and countries desperately anxious to modernize should be one of mutually beneficial partnership. The corporation gains access to new and growing markets, inexpensive labor, and sources of raw materials. The country, in turn, gets an infusion of technology, exposure to managerial expertise, training that builds up a cadre of skilled workers and experienced managers, and efficient use of its resources, since the corporation is responsive to market discipline."[10]

Sociocultural Impact

Like all hybrid expressions sharing the prefix *socio* (*socioeconomic, sociopolitical*) the term *sociocultural* indicates a malaise. This malaise is not unconnected with the fact that culture tends to be considered either as an unlimited territory covering all human activites or the whole of life or as the "fifth wheel of the coach," the variable that gathers together all the elements that could not be placed in the classification of other variables (economic, political, military, etc.).

I do not wish to open up a debate on this question. I have no intention other than to deliniate the relation between *culture* and *transnational firms* on the one hand and *cultural apparatus* and *transnationalization of the economy* on the other. I will give two definitions that can serve as permanent points of reference. The first comes from the French political scientist Maurice Duverger: "Culture is the set of techniques, institutions, behavior, life-styles, habits, collective representations, beliefs and values characterizing a given society." The second comes to us from the German, Jurgen Habermas, who sees the concept of culture in three sociological dimensions: *language, work, power*. These three dimensions define different functions of culture: an expressive function, communication, which makes possible social relations between the members of a collectivity; an economic function, adaptation (economic to the extent that adaptation covers the form of appropriation and reappropriation of nature); and a rhetorical function of legitimation or delegitimation, that is, that which allows the member of a collectivity to argue rationally the values implicit in the prevailing form of social relations.

Once these general references have been fixed, a lot of ground still remains to be covered to situate the notion of culture in this present stage of the development of transnational capital. Four essential angles of reflection can be envisaged.

Transnational Apparatus of Production of Cultural Commodities.

This corresponds to the emergence of a new phase in the phenomenon of the industrialization of cultural products and marks the advent of the hegemony of a culture whose principal vectors are the means of mass communication (press, radio, television, cinema, new communications technologies). This evolution in the cultural goods production apparatus, which we will factually analyze in the course of this investigation, can be grasped in the very evolution of concepts used in research since the end of the Second World War. First, there is the concept of *culture industry,* used by Adorno and Horkheimer, exiles in the United States from Nazism and present at the emergence of the power of radio, television and cinema in the 1940s.[11] In forging this concept, the two Frankfort school philosophers expressed their concern about the overall commoditization of culture production. According to them through an industrial mode of production, a serialized culture was obtained, standardized, and marked by the division of labour—a mass culture. The transformation of the cultural act into value abolished, in their eyes, its critical power and dissolved the traces of authentic experience. It was as philosophers that Adorno and Horkheimer pondered over the role of the creator and the role of an alternative culture, free of ties with technology. One had to wait until 1965 for the appearance of a more pragmatic concept, that of *knowledge industry,* clarified by the economist F. Machlup, more concerned with measuring the participation of this new industrial branch in the GNP than anathematizing the banalization of culture and the end of intellectuals' power.[12] It was under the umbrella of *knowledge industry* (the many knowledge producing machines, including communication machines) that some academics would regroup when they felt the need for an approach more economic than materialist. Some three years later, another German philosopher, Hans Magnus Enzensberger, completed the trilogy by fashioning the concept *consciousness industry.* This concept, however, was not for analytical ends but rather to denounce on the eve of the arrival of new broadcast technologies the incapacity of progressive forces to use the electronic media and their imprisonment within the "Gutenberg Galaxy."

With the marriage of the computer, telephone, television, cable, and satellite and the advent of telematic networks, a new arrival, the *information industry,* is likely to overtake "consciousness industry" and in the long run perhaps all the other designations as well. The concept of information industry was launched by Stanford University economists, who based themselves on the reality in their country ("the U.S. is now an information-based economy. . . . By 1970, close to half of the U.S. workforce was classified as 'information workers' ").[13] The concept *information industry* extends from *basic information* (all types of data-bank, financial, commercial, scientific, and technical information) to so-called *cultural information* (films, books, newspapers, magazines, telegrams, etc.) or again to the entire *know-how,* that is, patents, expertise, advice, management, and so forth. The ambitions of this concept know no boundaries as it is no longer only a question of circumscribing one aspect of industrial activity or marking off the frontiers of a scientific discipline but paving the way for a new society, the *information society,* which is succeeding the industrial society. If American researchers give this concept such standing, it is doubtless because they intend to establish thus the new status of information and knowledge (into which they incorporate cultural production in the strict sense) as a primordial factor of production, as a basic resource. Above all, the concept is seen as a new system of power, a new means of governing (although one needs avowals like that of the former advisor of Jimmy Carter and founder of the Trilateral Commission, Zbigniew Brezinski, to recognize this).[14]

The latest indication of a conceptual evolution can be noted in certain international bodies that speak less and less in terms of a culture industry in the singular but rather of *culture industries* in the plural.[15] These bodies, particularly UNESCO and the Council of Europe, are thus demonstrating their preoccupation with the fact that the so-called popularization of culture occurs more and more today through culture industries, most of which are transnational. Their importance is such that they challenge the traditional notion of cultural policy elaborated by nation-states. We are far from the eminently philosophical preoccupations of Adorno and Horkheimer. The present epoch belongs to social engineers and cultural planners, and research is characterized by the analysis of probable markets and the pursuit of social uses for the new technologies approaching. In order to develop overall policies in the cultural field, more and more nations (beginning with the European nations, which until now have been marked by a notion of culture on the fringe of its industrial definition) are beginning to recognize the necessity of knowing the functioning of these industries, that is, to analyse the diffusion process in its various phases (creation, conception, editing, promotion, distribution, sales to consumers), the structures of the industrial branches, and the firms' strategies. At the same time, they find it indispensable to reconsider state policies in respect to these industries.

Appearing recently around 1975, the concept *culture industries* has a field of competence not always clearly marked out by the organizations using it. This is illustrated by the various interventions at the colloquy on "the place and role of culture industries in the cultural development of societies," organised by UNESCO in Montreal in June 1980.[16] It is difficult to limit culture industries and mass culture to their media supports, as industries like tourism, for example, which can justly claim the title *culture industry,* are left aside. Furthermore, by concentrating the culture industries too exclusively in the leisure field, the powerful movement of rapprochement between the education apparatus and the entertainment apparatus or even the rapprochement between leisure, work, and education allowing the new communications technologies, is forgotten.

Business Practice as a Source of Transnational Culture

Alarmed at the lack of analysis in this domain, Karl Sauvant, in an article in which he tries to define the *modus operandi* of the so-called business culture, correctly notes, "This neglect is astonishing since foreign direct investment consists not only of capital investment but is usually accompanied by sociocultural investments. In fact, given the magnitude of international business, the prevailing pattern of close headquarters control over foreign affiliates, and the various linkages between foreign affiliates and host countries, the introduction of novel business values and behavioral patterns can be expected to have a profound impact on the cultural and social fabric of the societies in which international business is entrenched."[17]

To quickly qualify business culture, I would suggest it is a series of codes (and practices) governing the modes of work organization, production, circulation, and the exchange of commodities. They extend from codes governing the profile of the manager to those presiding over the establishment of public relations or the recycling of personnel or again the procedures for negotiation between partners (state, employees, trade unions etc.).

These codes apply as much to the forms of social relations internal to the enterprise as to those related to its external actions. A social microcosm, the enterprise is often the laboratory where macrosocial models are developed. To the forefront in the modernization of management methods of individual and group organization, the transnational enterprise is, often well in advance of the rest of society, the site where the first effects of the *techno-revolution* and the revolution of the productive forces take effect. As proof of this, I need only point to the transformation that communications systems are currently undergoing. The introduction of terminals and the computerization of banking networks to facilitate financial transactions but also to control clients and personnel surely constitute a heavy sociocultural investment in the preparation of mentalities for the installation of wider communications networks. The installation of such technology is legitimized naturally through notions like security, freedom of movement, efficiency, all of which allow the new model of social relations, reinforced under the cover of being a service, to be blurred.

The Transnational Firm as an Agent of Production of New Institutional Models

The impact of transnational firms cannot be analyzed in the 1980s in the same way as in 1970 or even 1974. The current economic crisis, at first announced as an energy crisis, has not turned out to be the conjunctural crisis that some had thought but very much a structural crisis, that is, a crisis affecting the very form of our societies. The present model of capital expansion is in crisis and needs other political, economic, and cultural forms to continue the accumulation process. What is in question is not only the way in which the world economy and national economies have functioned up to now but the way in which the political models that have served as their framework have evolved. As the Trilateral Commission recognised in 1975: "The more democratic a system is, the more likely it is to be endangered by intrinsic threats. . . . In recent years, the operations of the democratic process do indeed appear to have generated a breakdown of traditional means of social control, a delegitimation of political and other forms of authority, and an overload of demands on government, exceeding its capacity to respond."[18]

In the same way that we are seeing a redeployment of the mode of production of material goods, we are seeing an overall restructuring of the mode of production of cultural commodities. So-called mass culture or rather the industrialized cultural production apparatus, which is intertwined from now on with the main information production apparatus, is a political apparatus to the extent that one of its functions is to assure the adhesion of different groups and classes to a society's objectives. In other words, mass culture is not only a product of an industry but also an integral part of a political system. The fruit of liberal democracy and a project for the democratization of goods through the market and also the adoption of this project by different classes, mass culture is undergoing the metamorphosis and the challenging of the way in which democracy has unfolded up till now. This is to say that the culture industry, and in a broader sense the information industry, is increasingly considered in our societies not only as an economic way out of the crisis (notice that information has been set up as an essential factor of production, a basic resource), but equally as a political way out of the crisis (one no longer talks only of the information industry, but also of the information *society*). As a producer of consensus between groups and classes, as much at the national as at the international level, it is called upon to participate in the restructuring of attitudes or to use the words of Brezinski, who takes his desires for reality, to allow a "new planetarian consciousness" to be elaborated.

It is in this context that in the logic of their expansion, units of transnational capital contribute their quota in the remodeling of the means of social control (to use the expression of Michel Crozier, Samuel Huntington and Joji Watanuki in their diagnosis on the crisis of democracy).[19] The form of democracy proposed for tomorrow will be unlike that of yesterday. The shrinking of individual liberties will no doubt be mooted. This is the price to be paid for the maintenance of security, be it individual or collective, civil or military. Everything that still constitutes an obstacle to the growing integration of national economies in a world-wide schema and a new international division of labour is likely to become the preferential target of this remodeling. The principal targets are, without any doubt, the structures of the nation-state and all of its institutional apparatuses. The fruit of a historical heritage, these structures and apparatuses, in spite of the numerous contradictions running through them, remain in societies living under the civil sign of actually existing democracy, propelled by a series of norms and values that are in contradiction with the movement toward the transnationalization of economies. The production apparatus of cultural commodities and transnational information carries within it not only a cultural project, but also a new system of the organization of power. It is without doubt through this site of the commercial exchange of cultural commodities that the logic of transnationals tries to infiltrate in order to soften national resistance of all shades. Communication and culture occupy a prime place in the restructuring of institutional mechanisms insofar as what I would go so far as to call a privatization or commercialization of the state operates through them. This process involves the colonization of the state by commercial norms, necessarily more universalizing than norms of public service or public interest. The inherent pressure of the transnational model of expansion against everything relating to public functions must be read in this sense.

In all public sectors, one hears the call to delegate authority to the private sector, in response to a deep need for dismantling all networks of solidarity and for laying the foundations of a new, atomised society where everyone will be exclusively responsible for themselves, "the enemy being the next-door neighbour." Through these assaults on public functions that can be ascertained as much in the contesting of communications systems based on the principle of public service as in the attacks on the social security system established by the welfare state, a model of restricted democracy can be made out, another type of state. It is precisely against this new "democracy" project that those resisting this new interior order consistent with the new world-wide order are making a stand in countries where civil society as a site of expression and negotiation between social partners continues to function.

A country like Chile foreshadows the fact that this privatization scheme, which takes the monetarist theories of Milton Friedman together with his social model of overatomization to their logical conclusion, can only be established in developing countries under extremely authoritarian conditions, whereas it needs to follow more subtle paths in Western countries. As recently as January 22, 1981, *Business Week,* in its economic diary, reports that the government of General Pinochet has disclosed a plan for the privatization of the social security system (after having already set up a plan for the privitization of the education system). "One of the key problems facing the Reagan Administration will be to cope with the escalating cost of the Social Security system and its chronic financial instability. While there are no easy answers, the chances are that Reagan will propose some cutbacks in benefit levels, plus a change in the way benefits are indexed to inflation. The problem, of course, is that Social Security has a massive constituency that resists any changes in its operation. That, however, is apparently not a problem in Chile. The Pinochet government recently unveiled a plan to 'privatize' that nation's social security system. Workers are encouraged to set up their own individual accounts in private retirement funds. After five years, however, the new private system will become compulsory, and employees will have to put at least 10% of their gross salaries into their retirement accounts."

This privatization of large-scale social services, acquired by the Chilean working classes over the last thirty years, "changes the foundations of the social welfare system as it moves from being a method of redistribution to one of individual capitalization," as Santiago's conservative newspaper, *El Mercurio,* remarked on October 22, 1980.[20]

The transfer of communications technologies in developing countries (as in other countries) must be put into focus by taking this logic of privatization into account. The systems proposed by the transnational project contain not only a model for the modernization of the telecommunications system but also a model for the modernization of institutional mechanisms, for these technologies, by their very nature, are introduced in all spheres of institutional and private activity from education to hospital organization, including the rationalization of the judicial system and the production process. Once again, the notions of modernization, profitability, and efficiency could well hide the political stake in this new phase of the development of the commoditization of both the social and the cultural field.

If it is essential to continue asking ourselves how the public authorities can promote intervention policies and the regulation of culture industries of a transnational character, it is just as important from now on to ask ourselves how the growing strength of these industrial culture transmitters will be called on to strongly transform the fragile equilibrium between the private and public sectors for the formation of the necessary new consensus and therefore for the restructuring of the nation-state. The arrival of cultural products of transnational character must be studied just as much as new apparatuses of cultural production, which are installed in each national zone and correspond to the logic of transnational expansion. Does not the integration of national economies into the world economy in the current phase of transnationalization impose what would be, after a fashion, the "nationalization" of the matrix of transnational production or the localization of transnational models?

National/Transnational Articulations

One last question needs to be posed in order to describe what is meant by "sociocultural impact of transnational firms." There is too much of a tendency to set up transnational firms as the only actors in the transnational process consequently relegating the study of the national societies in which they are based to a minor level. What determines the particulars of this process in each national reality is the articulation of the proposals of transnational firms with those of the groups and classes that make up each national society.

Many rightly emphasize that in the analysis of the impact of the transnationals on developing countries, it is urgent to reestablish, for example, an analysis that considers the local bourgeoisies as social subjects and no longer as mere passive receptacles, mechanically reproducing the norms, values and signs of transnational power. Even if they are entirely subordinated to this transnational project, they can at least reformulate in accordance with the historical heritage and particular conditions the reception they give to these models, all of which profoundly influences the effect that the transnational cultural product is likely to have in each national territory. The process of transnationalization can only be understood in a complex correlation of national and international or even local and regional forces, crisscrossed by the existence of resistance, adaptation, recuperation, offensives, and mimicry.

This dialectical conception of exchange, albeit unequal, between the center and the periphery is in fact an open critique of a narrow conception, conveyed by certain representatives of dependency theory, that is marked by a regrettable tendency to economism.

Although recognizing the considerable contribution made by dependency theory, born especially in Brazil and Chile in the 1960s, Gonzalo Arroyo, a Chilean economist, sees in this economism the reason why the cultural field and resistance of popular classes has in fact motivated very little specific analysis on the part of these theoreticians. "The analysis of a historic process above all social movements at the base; the way in which they constitute, structure and express themselves; their ideological, cultural and religious dimension have been generally left aside by economists, sociologists, and other intellectuals identifying with the dependency current."[21] Trying to reconstruct the transnational phenomenon in a new perspective, he concludes, "This being the case, it seems that the only fertile path to follow, arduous and intellectually less attractive though it is, consists in deepening specific analyses of each country and reconstructing these analyses in a fairly fluid international context, extremely variable from an economic and political point of view. The category of dependence and the grid of analysis it contributed were undoubtedly useful, but they are no longer sufficient today. The external conditionings are just as numerous as the economic, social, and political realities of Latin American social formations; consequently possible roads to a solution are proving much more complex."

The growing malaise that is increasingly felt in the face of conceptual couples (which one must, however, continue to use in order to be understood) like center/periphery, industrialized countries/underdeveloped or developing countries, North/South, developed countries/Third World points to the need to go beyond analytical outlines to better grasp the realities of today. Such a revision is necessary not to proclaim the decline of ideologies, the end of the class struggle, or the end of the relations of force between North and South but, on the contrary, to insist on the permanence and the deepening of the relations of structural subordination and to better approach the transformation of modes of social domination at both national and international level in this new phase of the transnationalization process. In an interview in the French daily, *Le Monde* (December 20, 1980), the Brazilian sociologist Fernando Enrique Cardoso, director of one of the most important study centers in Latin America, the CEBRAP, and one of the leading figures of dependency theory in the 1960s, reminds us: "People go around repeating, 'for want of a revolution, there is underdevelopment.' In my opinion, this does not hang together. Who would deny that a deplacement between the center and the periphery, a dependence of one in relation to the other, exists? Is the periphery a united whole? Is even the concept 'Third World' operational? There are many ways for the periphery to be integrated into the center. It is history which supplies the elements for an explanation."

The succession of preceding citations illustrate the high level of critical research in Latin America. In the stock taking of sources available for carrying out this present study, it is certain that this subcontinent occupies a prime place. This is no doubt explained by two factors; the long history of the penetration of transnational corporations in Latin America, and above all, the existence of a resistance movement to the transnational strategy, materialized by social movements and processes as well as reflections on these realities. As Gonzalo Arroyo very rightly notes: "Most of this critical research, whether or not it claims to be Marxist, makes a choice in favour of the dominated classes. These researchers are engaged in social and political struggles, consequently breaking with an intellectual practice distant from the people."[22]

This brings me to a personal reflection. A study carried out mainly from existing sources like this one presents a serious problem, that of having to work with material that reflects different states of reflection and consciousness in the different regions and countries concerned. All the world's developing countries have not been able to construct concrete analyses from a lived situation, experienced as unequal and on occasions denounced as such by their political leaders. The density of research is extremely unequal according to different world zones. If Africa, for example, has given rise to prestigious researchers who are serious references for critical research in this continent for this specific domain of study, there are, however, far fewer studies compared to Latin America.[23] The reason for this disequilibrium cannot be explained merely in terms of the more recent transnational penetration because Unilever was already a pillar of colonization in Africa and Nestlé's entry dates back a long time. Critical groups from countries of the center often produce studies of the actions of transnational firms before the affected countries have been able to manifest their own reaction to the situation in the form of research and analysis. An example of this was the baby-killer scandal concerning Nestlé's actions in Africa, where a study and denunciation was undertaken by the Swiss group called the Berne Declaration Group. The existence or nonexistence of critical research in such and such a country is often the reflection of a more or less total state of dependence, sometimes maintained by local authorities with respect to the university apparatuses of the former colonizing countries or to the needs of transnational firms. As Edmundo Fuenzalida, analyzing the incorporation process of peripheral countries into the transnational system by using the expedient of science, notes, "To be accepted as a scientist it is necessary to perform research on the problems and with the methods that have been defined by the community of scientists in response to the demand of the main consumers (the multinational corporations and the military establishments of the central states). Therefore the institutionalization of research in a peripheral region means that some of its best talents will begin to work on such problems, with such methods, and not on new ones, of more relevance to the region. In other words, the local scientific establishment will grow to be a peripheric end of the transnational institution of science."[24]

Self-Reliance: Critique of a Model of Growth

The Ambiguous New International Economic Order

How does the notion of self-reliance challenge the notion of development and the growth models implicit in the logic of expansion of transnational firms?

Thanks to the crisis in the 1970s, both official and officious critiques of international development strategies were developed. Two levels of action that attempt to remedy the former growth model are currently combined to correct the reproduction of inequalities between the industrialized countries and the Third World. The first level concerns protest within international organizations. In respect to this, nonaligned countries demand a restructuring of international mechanisms to change the ground rules as regards commercial and financial exchanges as well as science and technology. This is to allow developing countries to industrialize and progressively put an end to the unequal distribution of world power. It was after their fourth summit conference in Algiers, September 1973, a little before the October decision of the OPEC countries, that the nonaligned countries ended up adopting during the sixth special session of the General Assembly of the United Nations two resolutions entitled, "Declaration on the Establishment of a New International Economic Order (NIEO)" and "Programme of Action on the Establishment of a New International Economic Order." Among the proposed measures were "commodities agreements" that tried to counter the deterioration of exchange, which has not been favourable to developing countries as producers of raw materials. Others were an unrestricted access to the markets of developed countries, greater financial flows, better access to IMF credits (the IMF being the most important credit institution of the international monetary system), special drawing rights, greater participation in the management of Monetary Funds, the establishment of a code for technology transfer, the establishment of a code of conduct for transnational firms, and finally measures facilitating the redeployment of industries to Third World centers.

Some have emphasised that even if these measures were carried out point by point, the NIEO could not lead by itself to a change in the structures of the international economic system. As Karl Sauvant pointed out in 1978:

> The answer is . . . that the structures of the international economic system would not be changed appreciably. On the contrary, they might even be further solidified. For the underlying philosophy of the NIEO program is essentially reformist; it is aimed at improving the existing mechanisms, not at changing the existing structures. Its main objective is to put the DCs [developing countries]—within the framework of the present system—in a better position to pursue their goals, especially to engage in trade and to participate in a "rational" international division of labour. The emphasis is on "put in position." The program basically represents—not surprisingly, one may add, in view of the training that many Third World leaders and experts have received in the academic centers of the industrialized core-countries—a liberal economic approach to the solution of the developing countries' problems. . . . In fact, a number of the key elements of the NIEO program have clear stabilizing effects on the existing international economic system; and in the long run, their implementation

may possibly even give the kiss of death to the pursuit of vigorous restructuring."[25]

The balance sheet drawn up by the French economist Georges Corm in *Le Monde Diplomatique*, November 1980 is scarcely encouraging. It goes so far as to say that "the international economic order is daily becoming more and more of a disorder that very few people, finally, have an interest in stopping." He continues, "One is confused by the number of international conferences monopolised by Third World officials and their main technical advisors, with hardly any results, whereas so many acute problems remain unsolved at the local level. It will not be at all surprising if the illnesses that the so-called developing countries suffer from are analyzed in terms of the international economy. This, in turn, facilitates a growing externalization of the Third World economy, whose functioning, submitted to increasing distortions, must depend more and more on modern technology that only transnational firms control at the international level."

In these conditions, the new international economic disorder becomes an easy way out for certain Third World leaders.

> In reality, proposals for the reform of the international economic order, whose list grows longer each year, aim more at assuring a larger and more stable integration of Third World economies in the dominant economy of the industrialized world than putting an end to a system of exploitation. One seeks to correct the most crying cases of injustice in the South as in the North to avoid even graver crises and eventual dangerous ruptures for the international equilibrium. The internationalization of "development" problems furnishes an extremely good alibi to Third World governments, thus in a position to invoke, faced with their frustrated population, the impossible reform of the international economic order that aborts internal development "efforts." For their part, governments of industrialized countries find easy material for public opinion with the increase of gasoline prices, immigrant workers, and the competition of new industrial countries. . . . This objective conjunction of interests between North and South elites does nothing to stimulate large-scale critical reflection on the errors of political economy of Third World governments.[26]

Self-Reliance as Strategy

The second level of activity that tries to avoid the equivocation we have just mentioned, proposes to link the pressure in international institutions in order to change the rules of unequal exchange, with a national development strategy breaking with the schemas of dependence on the international machinery. While recognizing the strategic importance of the struggle for the creation of the New International Economic Order (NIEO), the second level of activity establishes as a condition of existence for the NIEO and as a guarantee of the real emancipation of developing countries the necessity of constructing a development model adapted to their fundamental needs. Development begins to be envisaged, no longer as an externalization movement, whose motor of development is trade and transfers from the exterior, but as a process of mobilization of local resources with a view to satisfying local needs. It is in this context that the notion of *self-reliance* operates.

Dissatisfied with the way in which progress towards a new IEO is being carried out, some Third World countries are increasingly militating to incorporate this self-reliance strategy in the development programs of international organizations. In February 1979 the Group of Seventy-Seven, principal organization of developing countries integrated into the United Nations system, during the fourth ministerial meeting held at Arusha in Tanzania (a preparatory meeting for the Manilla UNCTAD session, May–June 1979), adopted a document with a particularly evocative title, "The Arusha Programme for Collective Self-Reliance and Framework for Negotiations." This shows these countries' desire to find an alternative, independent of the international market.

The first sign of the concept of self-reliance in an international institution can be found in the documents of the non-aligned countries Summit, held at Lusaka in 1970. However, rather than being a point of departure, it is already a point of outcome. In effect, it is already found explicit in the Arusha Declaration of 1967 by the governing party of Tanzani, TANU [Tanzanian Unity], seeking its own socialist model. In Chapter three of the Arusha Declaration, entitled "The Policy of Self-Reliance," one reads:

> The principles of our policy of self-reliance go hand in hand with our policy on socialism. . . . TANU believes that everybody who loves his nation has a duty to serve it by co-operating with his fellows in building the country for the benefit of all the people of Tanzania. In order to maintain our independence and our people's freedom we ought to be self-reliant in every possible way and avoid depending upon other countries for assistance. If every individual is self-reliant, the ten-house cell will be self-reliant; if all the cells are self-reliant the whole ward will be self-reliant; and if the wards are self-reliant, the District will be self-reliant, then the Region is self-reliant, and if the Regions are self-reliant, then the whole nation is self-reliant and this is our aim.[27]

However, if one needs to find a more distant place of origin for this notion, it is no doubt in the China of the Great Leap Forward that one must look. The basis of this movement was autonomy and self-reliance. In spite of the excesses and the manipulative practices that we now know of, the Chinese model of development, during this period, broke with all known socialist models and undertook an attempt to direct, as much as possible, key elements of Western technique to the masses by breaking with the monopoly of knowledge. Other socialist countries had maintained this monopoly by assuring the training of their technicians in the West. China refused to let herself be strangled by the financial and technological bottleneck and refused the industrialization strategy that was content to supply a small number of privileged factories with modern equipment, which, while increasing productivity, creates very little employment.

At present, the notion of self-reliance is endowed with an extremely large collective memory, as those who take their inspiration from it refer as much to Gandhi, Mao, Pablo Freire, or even Illitch as the Tanzanian experience or self-management socialism.[28] These influences mainly come from the Third World, intersecting in declarations of principle and speeches the experiments of social movements and groups in the developed countries denouncing the overexploitation of resources, the degradation of the environment, unemployment, social inequalities and overconsumption, industrialization, and urbanization patterns. These are demands that numerous international conferences on the environment, water, desertification, food, and so forth, have taken up these last few years. As an example, let us remember the Conference on the Environment in Stockholm in 1972 that insisting on the relation between the environment and development not only questioned destructive and inegalitarian development models but opened the way for the search of new development models, founded on a better use of resources particularly at the local level.

A series of declarations and programs have come to make explicit the strategy of self-reliance understood as the valuation of resources for the satisfaction of fundamental needs and as the local control of these resources. This was notably the case of the Cocoyoc (Mexico) Declaration in 1974, adopted by the participants of the Symposium on Models of Resources Utilization; A Strategy for the Environment and Development, organized by the United Nations Program for the Environment (UNPE) and UNCTAD. Part of this declaration reads:

> We believe that one basic strategy of development will have to be increased national self-reliance. It does not mean autarky. It implies mutual benefits

from trade and cooperation and a fairer redistribution of resources satisfying the basic needs. It does mean self-confidence, reliance primarily on one's own resources, human and natural, and the capacity for autonomous goal-setting and decision-making. It excludes exploitative trade patterns depriving countries of their natural resources for their own development. There is obviously a scope for transfer of technology, but the thrust should be on adaptation and the generation of local technology. It implies decentralization of the world economy, and sometimes also of the national economy to enhance the sense of personal participation. But it also implies increased international cooperation for collective self-reliance. Above all, it means trust in people and nations, reliance on the capacity of people themselves to invent and generate new resources and techniques, to increase their capacity to absorb them, to put them to socially beneficial use, to take a measure of command over the economy, and to generate their own way of life."[29]

The constituent aspects of a definition of self-reliance are the following:

1. Affirmation of the failure of a certain idea of development, of technical progress and industrialization, the revalorization of qualitative criteria to judge development, and the refusal to judge in terms of increasing the GNP. Here, the determination of fundamental needs appears; food, clothes, housing, education, self-fulfillment, participation, togetherness, and conviviality. All of these needs come back to dissatisfactions and frustrations provoked by linear industrialization strategies that assimilate social and human progress to industrial and technical advance wherein industry acquires a universal vocation as a method of harmonious development. These industrialization strategies have never taken into account the particularities of various groups making up a population or the specific contribution they could make in the drawing up of a balanced development policy.

2. Recognition of the value of solidarity. This is what serves as a basis for the idea of the participation of people in development in favour of everyone. In his preface for the first Mozambique journal of science and technology in August 1980, President Samora Machel wrote: "To learn is to advance together with the efforts of everyone, the contribution of everyone, and the participation of everyone so that all can progress permanently. To progress permanently is the duty of each person, and the progress of each person is the duty of everyone."[30] This requirement implies that development is conceived in terms of satisfying the *needs* of the entire population and not being content to respond to the *desires* of an elite or middle-class fractions. It can only be understood in a vast process of popular organization and the

political mobilization of the individual and the group. It can, therefore, only be conceived in a context of the overthrowing of social inequalities and their corresponding social structures. This solidarity, expressed through the realization of individual self-reliance, is also expressed through collective self-reliance at all levels: at the local level (family, commune, village federation, ethnic group); at the national and regional level (insisting more on relations with Third World countries than industrialized countries).

3. The notion of self-reliance is indissociable from the demand for cultural diversity and cultural identity. By challenging the notion of development pushed forward by the logic of transnational expansion, partisans of self-reliance support the demand for a cultural identity and their own cultural field as a site for political emancipation.

> Classical approaches to development have violated the first principle of human dignity, namely that human beings as well as their culture need to be treated by others with due respect, for their own sakes and on their own terms. Most agents of development however, have treated persons and cultures as mere instruments of economic growth or as variables to be manipulated to reach change targets. Cultural integrity is important because no one lives in a vacuum. All people inherit or adopt a culture, an integral whole of accumulated resources, both material and non-material, which they utilise, transform and transmit in order to satisfy their needs, assert their identity and give meaning to their lives. Culture is the source and the fulfillment of identity, meaning, survival, expression and dignity. . . . The vast majority of people in the Third World are rooted in cultures tied to a specific geographical area, a specific history, specific norms and values. These are the groups most vulnerable to the damage caused by the insensitive development strategies.[31]

Far from falling into culturalism, this same declaration dating from 1975 specifies that the term cultural diversity "does not mean chaotic fragmentation regardless of the consequences on national unity or world collaboration in solving vital problems. Nor does it mean 'freezing' present inequities based on caste, race, class and national privilege systems. The quest for cultural diversity would betray mankind were it to become any of the following: a retreat from shared global responsibility, isolationist parochialism, the rationale for turning threatened cultures into mere fossils to be preserved in some kind of social museum, game preserve, or mausoleum of the living dead."

4. By refusing to equate social progress with submission to the norms

of a certain development of technologies, the concept of self-reliance can only be understood in the light of a critique of technology transfer schemas. Judging these transfers as transplantations of power structures, this notion puts on trial the conception proclaiming the neutrality of technology, based on the idea that what determines the positive or negative character of its impact is solely the good or bad use made of it. The concept of self-reliance carries, therefore, a refusal of an *instrumentalist* conception of technology and poses the question of an appropriate science and technology designed for the fundamental needs of populations, notably their participation in the elaboration of science and technology. This is without doubt the most polemical point of the definition of self-reliance, giving rise to sometimes very divergent interpretations.

5. Self-reliant development is an invitation to developed countries to reconsider their own growth schemas. As the Cocoyoc declaration puts it:

> The world is today not only faced with the anomaly of under-development. We may also talk about over-consumptive types of development that violate the 'inner limits' of man and the 'outer limits' of nature. Seen in this perspective, we are all in need of a redefinition of our goals, of new development strategies, of new life styles, including more modest patterns of consumption among the rich. Even though the first priority goes to securing the minima we shall be looking for those development strategies that also may help the affluent countries, in their enlightened self-interest, in finding more human patterns of life, less exploitative of nature, of others, of oneself.

2
Principal Features of the Cultural Networks

Transnational Agents

Unequal Exchange

In 1977 a film that subsequently became well known, *Network,* was released. It was produced by United Artists, a cinematographic firm coming under a vast multinational conglomerate interested as much in aerial traffic, insurance, and credit as industrialized culture products. Showing that reality and fiction are becoming increasingly linked in the production of cultural commodities, this film represents Arab capital as an invading, autonomous, and all-powerful force. Will Arab capital go so far as to buy up one of the big American television chains? As Michèle Mattelart asks, "Is it possible that the Arabs intervene as a *cliché émissaire* in *Network* to dilute the idea of North American hegemony in television and world cinema?"[1]

One thing is certain: international investment always comes from a small number of agents. The share of the United States, the United Kingdom, Germany, Japan, Switzerland, and France increased on the brink of the 1980s to more than 80 percent of total stock. Admittedly, the power of American firms is no longer what it was in 1966. At that time there were eighty-seven enterprises in the world declaring an annual turnover of more than a billion dollars. Of these, sixty were controlled by the United States alone. A new equilibrium has been produced inside this group of powers.

Although United States direct investment in foreign countries still predominates, it has decreased in relation to the investments of other countries. As a percentage of outward direct investment of thirteen OECD countries, the U.S. share has decreased from a peak of approximately 60 percent during the 1961–67 period to about 30 percent from 1974–78. United States direct investment outflows were thus growing notably more slowly than those of other countries. Germany's share grew from about 7.2 percent to 16.7 percent; that of France from 6.9 percent to 7.8 percent, and that of Japan from 2.4 percent to 13.2 percent. In contrast the share of the United Kingdom declined somewhat from 8.7 percent to about 7.9 percent.[2]

These same Western countries have reoriented their investment flows toward the United States. The stock of foreign capital in the United States went from 9 billion dollars in 1966 to 41 billion in 1978. The United States thus reaped a quarter of net direct international investment flow over the period 1974–78 compared to 2.6 percent over the period 1961–67. As the economic analyst of *Le Monde,* Jacqueline Grapin, points out, investments taking place between developed countries strengthen their superiority. "Western investments in the Third World have increased, admittedly, in absolute value but less in relative value in relation to those remaining well and truly in the older industrialized countries. Above all, the growing number of investments between Western countries finishes by having a "gravitational effect" specific to their own region that reinforces still more their economic superiority."[3] If we believe the hypotheses of the Interfutures group of the OECD, the national revenue per capita in the United States at the end of the century will reach around $9,900 compared to $4,780 in 1980. The average European individual revenue will reach nearly $8,000 as against $2,450 in 1970. The average for the Third World will only be $900 per capita.

The number of host countries among the developing countries is proportionately limited. A small number of countries (Brazil, Mexico, India, Malaysia, Argentina, Taiwan, Hong Kong, the Philippines, Singapore, Colombia, and South Korea, to which Peru and Zaire must be added because of their mineral wealth) represented two-thirds of the stock of direct international investment located in non-European, non-OPEC, non-tax-haven developing countries. Countries like Brazil, South Korea, and Singapore are now classed by international organizations as *newly industrialized countries* (NICs). Third World unity is tending to disappear from statistical inventories.

In this context, the invasion of Arab capital is very relative. "A few statistics may help to place the widely discussed OPEC investment phenomenon in perspective. According to the Bank of England, of a total investment, cumulative, disposable OPEC surplus of $117.7 billion from 1975–8, only $1.3 billion was invested in the form of 'other sterling investments' including real estate and equities, or 1.1% of the total. The U.S. treasury has calculated that direct investments in the United States by oil-exporting countries equalled $228 million from 1974–8, or 0.6% of their total foreign investments in the U.S. during that period. The direct investment position of these countries in the United States at the end of 1978 was of an order of about 1/100 of 1% of total net worth of all U.S. firms."[4]

This distribution of transnational power is reproduced at all levels. Nothing is more normal than to find it equally at the level of cultural commodity production apparatus and more generally in the information industry. A statistic taken at random from a reading of *Business Week* concerning the service industry, where very different economic activities are regrouped: "In 1979, exports of services—insurances, engineering, communications systems, movies, banking and accounting—racked up about $36 billion for U.S. corporations. . . . In 1980, service exports were expected to hit about $45 billion and will be the major factor in generating a $2 billion surplus in the U.S. current account, the first since 1976."[5] This same article goes on to remark that "the potential world market for services, which has been growing at 15.7% a year for the past decade, versus a 6.7% growth rate for the merchandise trade, is enormous." In 1979, the United States continued to control 20 percent of the world services market, with France and Britain at around 9 percent each, Germany about 8 percent, and Japan a little more than 5 percent. (In 1973 Great Britain controlled nearly 12 percent and the U.S. 22 percent.)

At the more specific level of cultural commodities, even if at present a shifting in the relations of force is being carried out inside the transnational club and between this club and some newly industrialized countries, there has been no significant realignement established and the assertion of Brezinski in 1970 that the United States controlled nearly 65 percent of world communication flows is still valid for numerous sectors of the culture industries.

What are, roughly speaking, the characteristics of this club of agents? What is its structure? What is the extent of its international activity?

U.S. Matrix

Let us begin with U.S. firms. In the last two decades, the process of concentration has accentuated. We have seen the formation and reinforcement of vast cultural commodity production conglomerates (many of whom are otherwise integrated in diversified conglomerates that devote themselves to everything else but culture, like Gulf and Western, owner of Paramount; the publishers Simon and Schuster, and numerous record companies.)

Large hardware manufacturers have absorbed the centers of program development, educational messages, leisure formulas, or software. New entertainers and pedagogues are thus born. Can we still ignore, for example, that among the top ten world producers of the educational industry, one finds electronics giants, satellite manufacturers, media owners, Xerox, CBS, RCA, ITT, Westinghouse, General Electric, Litton and IBM?[6] The rapid development of new technologies only precipitates new alliances strengthening the hegemony of a few. All aspire to constitute the basis of the new "information society." As the directors of CBS made clear in 1980, "The plan to make the Publishing Group an Information Group became the core of a long-range plan to integrate the new technologies into the entire corporation."[7] We are seeing, in fact, an offensive from all sides, since the announcement of the arrival in the near future of satellites, videodiscs, fiber optics, and cable. The offensive of the large cinematographic companies in the direction of new communications technologies must be reconstructed within this framework. The large American film producers have made arrangments to launch the titles from their film libraries on new electronic markets. The remarks of CBS directors are once again relevant and cannot be expressed more explicitly. "We have the material from our books and magazines, and we can deliver it by slapping it onto a cable TV system or videodisc. We'll supply the software for whatever kinds of delivery systems come on the scene. . . . Now the technology is here, and it's important that we don't get left at the starting gate."[8] Let us remember that CBS, owner of the large television network of the same name, is a typical cultural conglomerate. Its revenues went from $2.2 billion in 1976 to $4.1 billion in 1981. Its activities range from paperbacks, educational material, records, the movie business, and electronic products to toys; its latest acquisitions are Fawcett Publications, the toy manufacturer Gabriel Industries, and *Family Weekly*. Recently, CBS has entered into a joint venture with Twentieth Century-Fox Films.

The pressure of large enterprises on cable television responds to the same desire to control not only production networks but also the distribution of new information products. Among the owners of the top ten cable companies in the United States (this form of television being expected to create another model for television), we find Westinghouse (which bought up the largest American cable network, Teleprompter, in 1980), Warner Communications (the cinematographic company that in association with American Express currently owns the fifth biggest network in the United States), the communications group Time Inc., CBS, another cinematographic firm United Artists and numerous large publishing firms.

The American business community scarcely seems anxious about the possible consequences such a concentration of interests might have on freedom of expression. Generally, this concentration is minimized through statistics that try to counterbalance an irrefutable diagnosis, ratified by numerous official commissions, of the interest of large enterprises to close ranks on the brink of the new information era. They are doing so without wanting to realize that what is important is above all the site where macrosocial use models for these communications technologies are constituted. This site can only be the hard core of the large enterprises mentioned. American Express had to propose a merger with McGraw-Hill, the biggest publisher of specialized and semispecialized magazines and one of the giants of the educational and information industry, to arouse protest in the business world. On this occasion, even *Advertising Age,* the mouthpiece of American advertisers, violently took sides against this takeover project.

> We are not against media mergers as such. While diversity is desirable, financial independence is important to an effective free press, and we recognise that mergers often bring fresh capital and know-how.
>
> But an American Express acquisition of McGraw-Hill would be something else. Nothing would be added. And at the same time control of some of the nation's leading business and industrial publications would pass from a management journalistic in its commitments to one which is concerned primarily with domestic and world finance.
>
> No assurance of independence for McGraw-Hill editors and publishers could overcome the inevitable suspicion that articles for *Business Week* and other M.-H. publications are shaded to serve the interests of American Express and the financial and industrial leaders on its board.
>
> The inevitable loss of credibility will vastly reduce the value of what American Express is purchasing. Among the other losers will be members of the American business community, who have been able to put their trust in these publications.[9]

These intersections in all directions (as, for their part, many large publishing houses are equally interested in audiovisual material or data processing industry) show the integration of the bulk of the culture and information industries, giving birth to multimedia conglomerates that in themselves span most sectors of cultural production, like Warner Communications, which is able to circulate its creations, not only through its publishing divisions (comics, posters, pocket books), its cinema division, its television division, but also through its video games and toy divisions. The merger between one of the world's biggest toy manufacturers, the American firm Mattel and Western Publishing, one of the biggest publishers of books and comics for children, in 1979 is one of the examples of this repetition syndrome that we have analyzed in a recent work.[10]

When different products of culture industries are not integrated in the same enterprise, they are found associated at the launching of a film or television series through new marketing strategies. The fashion for by-products that stimulates the unlimited reproduction of mass culture characters by means of the most diversified objects from toys to mustard jars has in the opinion of advertisers themselves considerably extended mass culture's sphere of activity. The film *Star Wars* gave rise to sales of more than $400 million in by-products in less than a year, whereas 160 firms have set themselves to launching 1,500 different products in the effigy of Superman. In the words of directors of the firms concerned, the ancillary rights for the film *Star Wars* "roughly double its take at the box office." As *Newsweek* confirms: "The super-marketing of Superman is a case study in the new economics of the Hollywood blockbusters. By most estimates, a film has to gross at least twice its production cost before it shows a profit. With a megabuck movie, that places a particularly high premium on non-theater sources of income-ancillary rights that can enhance a successful film or cushion losses on a bomb. 'The big change within the last four or five years has been the growth of all this ancillary income,' says Hollywood lawyer Tom Pollock. It's now a major, major consideration in the making of any movie.' "[11] The result can be seen in countries like Italy where in 1978 more than a quarter of the toy market came from television and cinema by-products with four star series, "Happy Days," "Sesame Street," "Heidi," and "Goldorak."

The outgrowth of distribution strategies quite naturally leads to new types of industrial alliance. From now on, Coca Cola will no longer simply serve as a vector for the heroes and themes of superproductions, but will start to produce these films itself. In January 1982 it took control of one of the last big pure entertainment companies, Columbia. Coke's directors made no attempt to hide the complementarity of the two corporations. "Purchase by Coke will undoubtedly mean additional funds, so that Columbia will be able to increase its production schedule significantly. Columbia is already respected for its distribution and marketing operations which would benefit from Code's marketing expertise."[12]

All this indicates that concentration breeds concentration, with many ways of reproducing itself. Even internal to the U.S. oligopoly of productions of cultural commodities, some are favored over others. "Today [1977] Universal Television (which belongs to MCA) produces more than 16 of the 63 weekly hours of prime-time television, including shows such as "Kojak," "Six Million Dollar Man," "Baretta," "The Rockford File," and NBC's Mystery Movies. Its nearest rival, Columbia, has only five hours a week."[13]

As far as the United States is concerned, let us draw attention, on the occasion of the setting up of large-scale communication technologies, to the fact that the interpenetration of the private and the public is being developed and reinforced. Witness the recent developments in the commercial satellite system (Satellite Business System), controlled by IBM allied to Aetna Life and to COMSAT Corporation. The latter is of a mixed character, a result of the permanent alliance subscribed to at the beginning of the 1960s by the U.S. government and the giant electronic firms like ATT, ITT, RCA and GTE Sylvania. Let us recall that COMSAT has also administered since its founding the international satellite system INTELSAT to which over 100 countries of the capitalist orbit belong.[14]

It is not by chance that large corporations from very different sectors are incorporating themselves more and more into the commerce of information. Along with several large financial institutions (Citibank, American Express), Exxon, the most powerful transnational corporation in the world, is a party to be reckoned with in this domain. Both natural and intellectual energy are being united in the same hands. Grey matter on the rise is uniting with the mythical black gold in retreat to consolidate its power. By the end of the 1980s, "the Exxon information companies could produce $15 billion in revenues. That may not amount to much in barrels of oil, but in advanced office systems, such volume would undoubtedly move Exxon to the top tier of vendors with as much of 10% of the market. By that time, the Yankee group expects that the total information processing industry will be worth $150 billion to $200 billion annually."[15]

The overall logic that pushes the developers of software towards the manufacturers of hardware and the owners of media towards the owners of other media is not exempt from contradictions. The trajectory of these mergers is sometimes halting, translating the trial and error and uncertainty that accompanies the creation of social uses for the new communications machines destined for the public at large or the institutional market. This tends to be illustrated by some of the efforts of IBM to move into the mass cultural production field. In 1979 in partnership with the multimedia conglomerate MCA-Universal, which contributed the technology of the videodisc, IBM founded Discovision Associates. MCA had developed the videodisc in its laboratories as well as building film library reserves; IBM, also long engaged in research on the videodisc, contributed above all its industrial production capacity and made available its immense distribution and marketing network. At the time Discovision spokespeople stressed that this type of joint venture, "will provide the opportunity to broaden the use of videodisc technology in the home entertainment and the industrial education and information fields."[16] In February 1982 MCA and IBM announced that they had decided to cede Discovision to the Japanese firm Pioneer Electronic Corporation, itself a partner of the Dutch firm, Philips. The reasons put forward by directors of the two firms affected to justify breaking off the contract: bad management, but also "the market just didn't develop fast enough." Some were not afraid to add that, "DVA tapped an IBM sales force skilled in selling computers—but lacking savvy in audiovisual gear."[17]

European and Japanese Cultural Industries

Is the horizontal and vertical integration model that tends to rule over the growth of the culture industries and in a wider sense, of the U.S. information industry, a scenario that is being installed in other countries, serving as a platform for transnationalization? It would be quick and easy work to affirm this point-blank, even if an image of exemplary competitiveness is attached to this model. Numerous factors prevent the mechanical reproduction of such a schema of interconnections: the different stages reached in the process of capitalist development; the status of public monopoly that takes in the whole radio-television apparatus, at least in the European countries; also the different relations between the intellectual or creator class and the institutions of power are undoubtedly some of the elements that any analysis must take into account. However, in these other countries also, the setting up of new communications systems is being prepared for.

It is in this context that in the European countries it seems necessary to reexamine the status of monopoly and public service in relation to the radio-television apparatus in the sense of a more commercial and privatized management.

France, whose resistance to a commercial conception of culture is legendary and reflects her historical heritage, has seen as recently as December 1980 the merger of hardware and software; the manufacturer of missiles, satellites, and rocket launchers, Matra, took over the large publishing group Hachette, thus attempting, as the managing director of Matra indicated, "to create, for the first time in France, an industrial group in which both container and contents are going to be able to merge on a large scale." The protests and commentaries of the Parisian press were in agreement on many points. To take one at random, *Le Matin:* "With the seizure of the Hachette group by Matra and the Bank of Paris and the Netherlands, the first French conglomerate of 'communication' is born. It is probably the most important event of the year. It is going to condition everything affecting the formation of attitudes, opinions, and fashions. . . . It is not impossible that Giscardian France will orientate towards a single-headed communication and information system in the name of economic efficiency. It is true that newspapers are enterprises. But it is also true that concentrations are particularly fraught with consequence here. The pluralism of the press is today endangered."[18]

The nationalization of Matra after the socialist victory in France in May 1981 has considerably limited the scope of this merger. However, it has not done away with the logic of mergers between hardware and software manufacturers. In the meantime other mergers have resulted, such as that bringing together the publishers Gallimard and the cinema firm Gaumont. This alliance, it must be recognized, looks more solid than the marriage between Coca-Cola and Columbia and shows that national factors intervene in this new phase of concentration with all the weight of their historical tradition. An unknown factor remains: what will be the behaviour of the ousted owners of the large French industrial groups towards the information industry, keystone of economic power tomorrow and political battleground today?

It is also time for consolidation in the Federal Republic of Germany. At its head is a family publishing empire, Bertelsmann Corporation, the second largest publishing empire in the world, only exceeded by Time. With its basic products (book clubs, magazines, book publishing, printing, records and promotional films), Bertelsmann declared a turnover of $2.2 billion in 1979, compared to Time's $2.5 billion. Unlike Hachette incorporated into a group of satellite manufacturers and other communications technology, Bertelsmann has scarcely left the orbit of message making. But in order to expand, it has decided to cross the Atlantic. Since 1977 it has taken over Bantam Books; *Parents' Magazine;* launched an edition of *Geo*, a direct competitor for *National Geographic;* established a subsidiary of Ariola Records; founded a book club; and taken over printing houses. All of this after having reinforced its position in its headquarters and throughout the European Community.[19]

Great Britain is undoubtedly the European country where cultural commodity production is the most integrated. As the British researchers, Graham Murdock and Peter Golding recall after having listed the twelve principal enterprises in 1977: "All twelve of the companies listed in the table appear in the *Times* list of the top 350 industrial companies in the economy, ranked by turnover, and the first four in the table figure in the top 100 (The *Times* 1000: Leading Companies in Britain and Overseas 1975–6, *Times* Books). In short, communications is big business. . . . The majority of the leading communication companies are diversified conglomerates which get anything from a half to two-thirds of their turnover from activities other than their main sector of operations. EMI for example gets 51% of its turnover from its music division, 31% from electronics manufacture, and 12% from commercial television programming."[20] In 1979, EMI itself was taken over by Thorn Electrical, one of the rare British television manufacturers not to fall under Japanese control. The takeover of the venerable *Times* by the Australian financier Rupert Murdock is one indication among many others that in Britain, many things are happening at the level of the restructuring of the culture industry. The latest illustration is the invasion of American publishing houses, which, for example, have seized 20 percent of the British university textbook market as against 7 percent in 1970, and the competition for markets in the former British empire. In India, for example, "the British used to command 90% of the English-language market. Now they have only 50 percent, and the U.S. has taken 40 percent."[21]

Japan, according to many people, occupies in the new international division of labour in the audiovisual field a prime place in the domain of electronic production for a mass public (radio, hi-fi, television, video recorders, calculators) to such an extent that one already wonders whether consumer electronics is not *de facto* reserved for Japanese transnational firms. In spite of the Orderly Marketing Agreement that limits Japanese exports to the United States to 1.7 million television sets a year, as against 3 million in 1976, the American market is still largely dominated by Japanese products. At this pace, as American analysts predicted, the future of American TV manufacturers will be very problematical. The American consumers electronics companies that have lost the battle over the Japanese video-recorders are now in a weak position to guarantee the hegemony of their videodisc. Meanwhile, European TV manufacturers are currently undergoing a total restructuring to face up to the same Japanese competition. Japanese companies supply 75 percent of Europe's hi-fi gear, 10 percent of its color TV sets, 30 percent of its picture tubes, and 80 percent of its video-recorders.[22]

One would have thought that this offensive and specialization would have been accompanied by a tight alliance between equipment firms and cultural commodity manufacturers, but there is nothing of the sort. The Japanese are suffering serious difficulties in finding programs in order to sell their videodiscs. (For the launching of the Japanese JVC videodisc in the United Kingdom, Thorn-EMI is supplying all the software for the discs and is offering at least two different films and programs.) The shortage is doubtless one of the reasons since a short time ago, the Japanese seem bent on constructing a veritable transnational cultural industry, which, profiting from the slot still available in the world market, could accompany their video-cassettes, videodiscs, and so forth. Clearly Japan, with an annual average of four hundred films, is already one of the largest cinematographic producers; but her sphere of influence in this respect scarcely extends beyond the Asian orbit. In the last five years, the firm Toei-Doga, profiting from the lack of supplies in the domain of mass cultural productions for children, has succeeded in lifting itself up to the highest ranking for world production of cartoons, with series such as "Goldorak, "Albator," "Heidi" and many others. An interview with the founder of Toei-Doga throws some light on Japanese projects. "From the end of this year [1980], we can begin production of the first televised series in which the computer has done the drawings, colouring, and direction. This system is going to lead to an considerable reduction in production costs, and above all, a phenomenal improvement in productivity."[23] Already, many people are predicting: "There are innumerable producers of cartoons, many production houses, and many products. European industry cannot even consider a fight on the same grund and even North American industry is endeavoring, in vain, to maintain its place."[24]

One burning question: does this competition, internal to the central countries, give rise to a diversification of messages on the international market? Few researchers or political officials have looked into this question. It touches a thorny issue: what is becoming of national cultures in the central countries linked to the transnational system under U.S. hegemony? Several years ago, I noted in relation to European countries that dominant national cultures in the transnational era must not only assure the reproduction of the dependence of the local bourgeoisie in respect to the United States, but also the reproduction of their hegemony as a dominant class in a determined nation, that is, to continue to sustain themselves as an "internal bourgeoisie," in the apt expression of Nicos Poulantzas.[25] For fear of seeing their legitimacy undermined, local bourgeoisies are forced to reformulate their hegemony within their national territory. In the political framework of an integration into the international system, European bourgeoisies, increasingly trans-nationalized, do not appear to offer serious alternatives to American hege-monic models of mass culture production. At the most, they give a local colour to matrices recognized as universal. Too often, this American model is simply accepted as being the last word in modernity, or even, to use the words of Jean-Louis Servan-Schreiber (brother of the author of the famous *American Challenge,* which was little more than a plea to let Europeans Americanize themselves), the "realm of intelligent capitalism."[26] The fas-cination for American management methods, human relations, and maga-zines is the recipe that has succeeded in giving a singular style to the press group owned by Servan-Schreiber. This is one element of a reply, but there are others. The importance of the working class movement and the new social movements in countries like Italy and France (especially since the victory of President Mitterand) allow one to suppose that this installation of American norms under the cloak of transnational modernity is not nec-essarily accepted. This is so even if these workers' movements that continue to weigh heavily on the functioning of these societies are, until now, hardly concerned about culture and its content in their demands and struggles. It is certain, for example, that there are more contradictions between capital and labour in a French news agency like AFP, compared to AP and UPI in the United States.

This said, the recent history of Japanese penetration in the domain of cartoon production indicates an undercurrent in the production of cultural commodities for a transnational public; namely, the interchangeability of messages. As a French educator notes: "Goldorak is a Japanese hero who has wiped out his origin. He is from everywhere, that is, Western, because one knows that the only particularisms are amongst the dominated (Bretons in France, the French in Europe, and the Europeans in the West, i.e., in the American orbit). Goldorak and Albator are, therefore, at the same time products of a world where the rule is to yield to the dominant model (the white model) and the combattants for an industry that knows that in order to survive, the *whole Western* market must be conquered and in order to do this, standardized (characters as well as cars)."[27] Another question which must be asked is that of the possible repercussions for their European fiefs in the qualitative leaps undertaken by firms like Bertelsmann and Hachette, for example, by investing and learning to produce in the United States. The same question must also be asked in respect to the multiple links woven between transnational hardware and transnational software, as the alliance between MCA-Universal and the Dutch firm, Philips, for the videodisc illustrates.

Before moving on to an analysis of the internationalization of the production and circulation of commodities, let us add one last item to our dossier on multinational interconnections; the high internationalization of shareholders and loan financiers. As a French economist mentions: "Philips's capital in 1970 was divided up as follows: Netherlands 47 percent, United States of America 13 percent, Switzerland 19 percent, France II percent, England 4 percent, and Germany 3 percent. Japanese shareholders only own 55 percent of Sony's capital, the rest being divided between the United States 38 percent, and Europe and Southeast Asia 17 percent. Matsushita is quoted at seven foreign stock exchanges, and so forth. This international financing of large multinational firms, also found in a number of long-term loans, comes back to the fact that in the industralized countries, national capitals finance the major part of the investment of foreign firms."[28]

Transnational Networks of Cultural Commodities

Let us now attempt to extricate the principal networks through which cultural commodities circulate—film, television, advertising, publishing products, education, and tourism.

Film Network

This is undoubtedly the culture industry branch that was the first to internationalize not only in respect to distribution but also production. It is also undoubtedly the first media that U.S. firms controlled overseas. All this had already begun in the 1920s. However, at that time, when coproductions were arranged with France, for example, films were totally integrated into the local culture. The strength of the American cinema firms and their integration into a vanguard sector of a whole life style is fully recognised. As this already dated declaration by the President of the export cartel, MPEAA (Motion Pictures Export Association of America), points out, "As far as I know, the cinema industry is the only branch of American industry which deals with foreign governments on equal terms." The power of this cartel has earned it the nickname, *mini state department*. What has become of it today? According to the statistical directory of UNESCO published in 1977, imports in terms of the number of films represented in 1975 from a sample of seventy countries, more than 90 percent of the total consumption in forty-eight countries, and from 70–90 percent in fourteen others. Only the United States, the USSR, Japan, India, and Korea watch more national films than foreign ones. Finally in France, Italy, and Pakistan, importation and national production are evenly balanced. The United States with 32 percent of its films exported occupies first place among exporters on the international market.[29] Most of these films come from eight large groups: MCA-Universal, Warner, United Artists, 20th Century Fox, Columbia, Paramount, Walt Disney, MGM.

Thomas Guback has clearly shown that if American films only supply 32 percent of imported films and only represent 5 to 6 percent of world full-length films, they take in half of world receipts.[30] India, one of the largest world film producers (between 500 and 800 a year compared to 150–250 a year for the American industry), cannot match such a performance on the level of receipts, even if in East African countries, it largely dominates the local box office. North American world takings can only be explained by the maturity of its international distribution and marketing networks. It is there that one understands more clearly the extent to which it is difficult to abstract the strength of a culture industry from the economic system from which it stems and which constantly propels and relaunches it . "We know," an MPEAA official has asserted, "that motion picture and television programs are one of the most effective means of creating demand for American goods in foreign markets. When attractive U.S. products are seen on the screen, it generates an immediate demand for them which benefits other American export industries."[31] New marketers of the film industry have understood this very well through their sponsoring and launching strategies for by-products, combining the strike force of Coca-Cola networks, for example, with the publicity posters for *Star Wars*. This is what has happened recently in Mexico.

It is perhaps through the cinema industry that we can understand more clearly the necessity experienced by the large transnational conglomerates to be present at every moment in their consumers' existence. The advertisements of LCA, the licensing division of Warner Communications, extol the advantages to be obtained through linking comics, films, television, and the promotion of consumer goods."

"Everything's stage center when your product is identified with DC super-heros. Because DC super-heros are up front with the public. In movies, comics, department stores, and on TV, Batman and Robin are currently being viewed on network TV in the "New Batman Show" . . . so are Super Friends and Shazam. And Wonder Woman has her regular series on the CBS network in prime time. Constant exposure combined with timely promotion has helped Super Heroes in their *fight for truth, justice and sales* [emphasis added]. Already LCA, the licensing organization representing the DC Super Heroes, is helping stores catch on the cape-tails of the new Superman movie. With full color display of Superman as he appears in the film and a series of action display pictures.

The film industry and more generally the television industry play here the role of locomotive to which the most diverse cars are hitched up; one thinks of the incredible sales of a single record, *Saturday Night Fever,* with over 38 million copies sold worldwide, over half in overseas markets. However, one thinks above all of the toy industry, directed at one of the favorite clienteles of transnationals—children. A single example suggests a field of study extremely neglected. In 1977 dolls, soft toys, toy cars, electronic games, and toy guns (in decreasing order of importance) represented more than 80 percent of sales on the Mexican market. Three firms shared 60 percent of these sales. All three were subsidiaries of franchises of American transnationals: Lili Lady, bought up at the end of the 1960s by the American firm General Mills, alone accounts for 25–35 percent of the market; the second, CIPSA, holds the Mattel franchise and 20 percent of the market with it; finally Plastimarx, responsible to Fisher-Price, a division of Quaker Oats, holds 10–15 percent.[32] When one knows that the toy industry is increasingly linked to the medias ("The toy industry's reliance on character merchandise has increased dramatically in recent years," said a special survey published in the *Financial Times,* December 28, 1977,) one becomes more aware of the fundamental role it occupies in the tango between cultural commodities and their child audience. Superman, Starsky, Batman, James Bond, and Barbie, without forgetting the older Disney characters, are all in these firms' catalogs; they are the characters portrayed the most on dolls, mascots, and toy cars. It is these characters that take children by the hand to introduce them to the world of electronic gadgets.

Let us return to the cinema proper. India is a paradigmatic case, but it is not the only peripheral country to have been able to mount a capitalist cinema industry. Mexico is one of these other countries. Forty years ago, Hollywood, owing to the war, favourised the strengthening of the Mexican cinema to the detriment of the two other poles of Latin cinema, Argentina and Spain, in order to find a platform for the antifascist offensive. Today, however, the Mexican national industry faces immense problems. In 1979 out of 435 films on first release in the metropolitan zone (Greater Mexico City,) 154 came from the United States, 79 from Italy, 23 from England, 18 from Spain, 16 from France, and 78 from Mexico. In other words, 35 percent of films launched in the zone were American and 82 percent were foreign. Of films on first release in the metropolitan zone, 29.7 percent were distributed by four transnational firms (Columbia, 20th Century Fox, Warner, Cinema International Corporation); 28.7 percent were distributed by medium-sized companies whose distribution was 95 percent foreign films. National films were distributed by companies which devoted 90 percent of their distribution to national material. As a group of Mexican researchers have clearly remarked, the transnational companies have played a not inconsiderable role in the working out the programing for individual cinemas.

> These distribution companies have succeeded little by little in taking over daily more cinemas not only in the metropolitan zone but equally in the large cities of Mexico. They take over the best cinemas, frequented by the middle classes, thus reducing the potential market for national firms, which find themselves relegated to cinemas in the working-class suburbs of large cities and most of the cinemas on small towns and villages. The latter adopt them as their "natural" cinema because of their illiterate audience with little spending power. This partly explains why national films have never succeeded in doing what other film industries succeed in every day, namely to recoup their investment within their national boundaries.[33]

As these researchers point out, this only partly explains the hegemony of foreign films. In other sections of their study, they rightly mention the weight of the tastes created in certain social categories. In 1976, 96 percent of the category of industrialists, bankers, merchants, and all those with a monthly income of more than fourteen thousand pesos, preferred foreign films; 68 percent of the "middle class" category (about 36 percent of the population) also preferred foreign films, whereas 71 percent of the lowest income group (less than five thousand pesos a month) preferred national films.

Sidney Sokhona, an African filmmaker, has the following observation on the situation of national cinemas in French speaking Africa: "Throughout this part of Africa, except for three or four countries that have recently nationalized their distribution circuits, any African filmmaker living in Africa who gets around to making a film is forced, if he wants to have it distributed in his own country, to go through Paris and propose it to SOPACIA, a subsidiary of UGC France." UGC France, a cultural conglomerate, dominates the production and distribution of films in France. Continues Sokhona:

> The countries that have nationalized their cinemas lack the means and still stock up with SOPACIA. Still worse, in Senegal where the state, having nationalised the cinema, owns 80 percent of the shares and SOPACIA the other 20 percent, the 20 percent have more power than the 80 percent, as SOPACIA above all does not want to be threatened with or have competition between Western and African films in Africa. Its extra strength comes from owning the cinemas, seats, and machinery in many African countries (and empires). . . . For fifty years, the same films have been seen on African screens, films scarcely seen in the West. They are the worst imaginable rubbish: *Django, Ringo,* Indian films or karate films, without forgetting the unforgettable *Tarzan!* As for the few African films seen on African screens, one cannot deny they have been profitable. In 1975 Sembene Ousmane's *Xala* beat all records for takings in Senegal, surpassing *Operation Dragon* (with Bruce Lee), confirming the idea that even if our people are accustomed to escapist films, our own films interest them and that a deliberate, concerted policy is condemning us on our own ground."[34]

In other countries, such as Thailand, for example, where the film industry is practically nonexistent, the only existing brake on the penetration of Western films (mainly American) is the competition from Hong Kong or India (29 percent of Thai film imports from 1961–76, compared to 32.4 percent for American films, and 6.5 percent for Japanese films).[35]

The general feature of the transnational film industry is the strong internationalization of distribution circuits. At the level of the internationalization of products, cases of coproductions with Third World countries are rare. Even when one comes across one of these rare cases, participation in the conception and direction is still more rare, for the rule is to confine the participation of the local people to the playing of extras; compare, for example, *Godfather II* from Paramount, which provided 880 temporary jobs to people in the Dominican Republic living in territories belonging to Gulf and Western, the owner of Paramount. Does this mean that the problem of the international target is not an issue for these companies when it is a question of approaching overseas markets? At the distribution level, transnational firms have worked out specific distribution strategies. As Warner Communications, Incorporated (WCI) put it in their 1975 annual report, WCI has elaborated a specific international distribution strategy. According to them: "Applying domestic release patterns is impossible when dealing with as many markets as there are regions and cultures. Warner Bros representatives must be diplomats, economists, union negoticiators, specialists in import-export regulations, and tax and censorship experts. Also, in order to give each firm the individual (marketing) attention it requires, they must be kept fully appraised of each movie from pre-production to the arrival of the picture in their company."[36]

For American firms the biggest market remains the internal one, and it is only very rarely that it dawns on them to conceive of films for an audience other than an American one. The crisis of Hollywood in the early 1970s resolved by the absorption of the majors into various conglomerates, was one of those privileged moments where the North American film industry could be seen doubting itself and coming to terms with the idea that from then on it must make films for specific audiences. A long investigation of U.S. cinema firms in 1973 reads: "Meanwhile, moviemakers are getting only 33% of their total revenues from overseas, compared with a time-honoured 50% year after year. To recapture foreign moviegoers, some U.S. companies are starting to make films abroad for specific geographic markets. MGM, for example, will make six movies in Europe to be shown only in Europe. Warner Bros. has made three movies in Italy and three in France for European distribution. When United Artists made *Last Tango in Paris,* it planned distribution only in Europe. Not until the film received rave reviews at French film festivals did UA decide to distribute it worldwide."[37]

This preoccupation, which, in any case, never went beyond the audiences of developed countries, quickly vanished from the horizon with the recovery of American films, which were increasingly proposed as the *international film* par excellence. The problem of national audiences disappeared in the same movement. Interviews with officials of American majors at the Cannes Festival in 1977 make this point very clearly. When the president of United Artists was asked to compare the profitability of films made in Europe with those made in the United States, he replied: "If you talk in pro rata terms they are very much on a par, that is if you talk about investment against return. If you talk in terms of real raw dollars, naturally European films are much more difficult to market internationally because they're made for a much narrower mentality. American firms are *by nature* international [emphasis added]. I think that grew out of the years when at one time the

American film industry was really dominating the world, which it doesn't really today. But since you can market an American film on a broader basis in terms of raw dollars, American films bring us more money." The president of Warners hammered home the same point. "I think also that in France, like in Italy, the filmmakers have started to realize that you cannot make a picture anymore that is typically French because your costs are so high that if you don't have an international picture—a truly international picture—you're bound to lose money. You can do very well in France, relatively speaking, but you still don't recover your investment. I think that is one of the most important lessons that is going to be learned now, especially in European areas that have a motion picture industry, such as France and Italy."[38] In 1977 on the basis of Jack Valenti's figures, the foreign cinema market produced 4.5 percent of the total U.S. cinema rental income. The foreign TV market represented 23.4 percent of the total TV market.

In the search for the international film par excellence, strategies of production that unite the widest and most transnational consensus possible are arising. On the occasion of the release of *The Wild Geese,* a sanguinary tale of mercenaries taking on an African dictator, several norms for the "global film" were unveiled. An analysis in the *New York Times* reads as follows:

> . . . It represents the latest example of the film designed to have international appeal, even at the risk of diminished acceptance in the United States. . . . The so-called "global-oriented" film has several noticeable traits. Its cast is chockablock with big-name stars, usually of several nationalities. But the Lorens and Burtons and Caines who find themselves so prominently billed in films of this genre are rarely called upon for a tour de force of acting; three dimensional characters depend on good dialogue, the nuances of which are lost in translation. And translation is what these films must excel at, so witty repartee, even by the likes of Neil Simon, is definitely out. Instead, the stars tend to serve as foils for action; they exist to shoot and get shot. For global films are also engineered to play heavily on the elemental magic of the medium; grand actions against exotic backgrounds. Mayhem and carnage need no subtitles.

Taking this reasoning to its logical conclusion, one of the directors of the British firm EMI added "We won't make a picture that we feel won't sell foreign. We don't make our pictures exclusively for peasants, but we want our films to be understood by—I want to use a decent term—a semi-literate person in Uruguay, so we can sell it in Uruguay."[39]

Are other international film industries, like Hong Kong's for example, preoccupied by the same problem? Some Hong Kong studio practices, like those of the Shaw Brothers Company, would seem to indicate that several versions of the same film are adapted for different clientele. Speaking of pornographic films, the Shaw Brothers Company explains, "We shoot in three versions: mild for Singapore; half-and-half for Hong Kong; and all-the-way for foreign."[40]

We have insisted on the case of the cinema industry and specifically on the question of targets of an internationalization process, because it allows us to take on questions, which, with different force, are posed in different sectors of the culture industries. The articulation of the national and the international can only be understood in the light of the balance of power in each sector or even each historical period. This is shown by the slightly opportunist reaction of cinema firms that, at the time when their fortunes were at their lowest ebb, were the first to proclaim regional particularities.

The arrival of new technologies (in particular the videocassette and videodisc) could make the situation worse for countries lacking a national cinema industry and strengthen the superfluous hegemony of American cultural conglomerate. A number of peripheral countries are already faced with this situation. At the end of 1979, one industrialist estimated that already "nearly 250,000 of the 1,700,000 videotape recorders now in consumer homes worldwide can be found in ten oil-rich Arab nations. About 150,000 of these 250,000 represent 1979 sales."[41] Moreover, it is estimated that of the 1,000,000 units sold in the United States since 1975, "about 160,000 . . . have since been shipped for resale to Venezuela (an estimated 100,000 units), Columbia (40,000) and the Caribean (20,000)."[42] Most of these players entered illegally or on the very borderline of legality; their numbers were such that in order to know the total number of units in circulation in these countries, those entering legally would have to be tacked on. U.S. software manufacturers have elsewhere demonstrated their concern for these illegal practices, for piracy also extends to programs." Addressing the software piracy problem, this sale of unauthorized tapes is most prevalent in the Middle-East, South Africa, Colombia, Venezuela, the Caribean and the South China Sea regions, where native TV programming and movie theater fare are minimal. The Middle East is a 'helluva market' for both hardware and programming sales . . . 4,000,000 program cartridges will have been sold in the Middle East through year's end. Indeed, the 2,000,000 software cartridges sold during 1979 alone . . . will represent 10% of the 20,000,000 software cartridges likely to be sold around the world in '79. Most of these sales in the Middle East are illegal, since piracy is rampant there. . . . About

300 or more companies distribute feature films, TV programs and other fare in non-U.S. markets after these properties have been copied from over-the-air TV stations and pay-cable systems, chiefly in the U.S."[43] Among the 6,000 to 8,000 titles available: *the Deer Hunter* (which had just been released!) *Turning Point, High Anxiety, Force 10 from Navarone* (barely a month after their U.S. broadcast or cablecast).

Television Network

According to the now classic study by the Finnish sociologists, Nordenstreng and Varis in 1972, French and British exports of TV programs reached a volume of twenty thousand program hours each; those of the German Federal Republic were estimated at six thousand hours, whereas the total for North American world exports varied between one hundred and two hundred thousand program hours.[44] In the peripheral countries, excluding exceptional cases like Mexico, already a program exporter at the time, very few countries could boast of any exports whatsoever. According to the same source, Latin America, with only 3 percent of the world's television sets, received approximately 35 percent of American program exports. The result: an average of 40 percent of the region's programing was North American. In Guatemala this proportion could reach 80 percent at times. In many other countries, South Korea for example, there are similar levels of dependence. Today a series like "Kojak," produced by MCA-Universal, simultaneously reaches audiences in over a hundred countries, whereas a French production sold overseas generally does not circulate in more then ten countries. The MIP-TV at Cannes (the stock exchange for TV programs) in 1979 confirmed the supremacy of Anglo-Saxon producers; if the Americans remain the uncontested masters of the series, then the Japanese and the Eastern bloc shine in cartoons, and the French and West Germans shine in musical programs. Great Britain, whose exports have increased substantially since 1972, excelled in background news reports, and the Scandanavian countries in documentaries, whereas Italy continued with its policy of tele-cinema coproductions.[45] Consultation of the public and the choice of themes to suit national audiences scarcely counts in the TV series industry whose dynamics are given over to exports. The series heading the ratings correspond to the tastes of the American market that allows producers to recoup 75 percent of their production costs. That which triumphs on American channels lays down the law in Paris, Rio, and Tokyo. The choice made by each channel in purchasing countries conforms to the dynamic given by the applaudometers of the

American metropolis, as only those series having triumphed on the screens of CBS, ABC, NBC get to the external markets. (Thus, three out of ten new series launched on American channels in September 1975 were banished from them by the following April.) Translation into foreign languages creates, in turn, other chains of dependence. The selection made by French channels and the adaptation in Paris by dubbing firms engaged by subsidiaries of American companies, constitute in their way so many relays of dependence to their peripheral French-speaking countries. Since 1972, however, attention must be drawn to the substantial change on the Latin American continent where *telenovelas* from Venezuela, Brazil, Mexico, Miami and Puerto Rico now occupy a dominant place in the ratings and constitute serious competition for North American series.

In the domain of news-film agencies, nothing counterbalances the importance of the three large companies dominating the world market: Visnews (United Kingdom), UPITN (United Kingdom/United States), and CBS News (United States) to which ABC News (United States) and DPA-Etes (West Germany) must be added. Visnews, the largest of these transnational agencies, owned by the BBC, the Canadian CBC, the Australian ABC, the New Zealand NZBC and the press agency Reuters, has a network of 190 subscribers and according to its own figures, covers 99 percent of the world's television sets. UPITN, owned by the British commercial channel ITN and the American press agency UPI, sends film news to more than one hundred foreign television stations from their offices in London, New York, and elsewhere.[46]

However, one of the most determinant elements linking the national radio-television systems to the transnational system is the genealogy of their installation. No peripheral country has escaped from the influence of metropolitan styles; the commercial, audience-maximizing American model, or the state monopoly model particular to the two former colonial powers, France and Great Britain. This is the case even if the particular characteristics of each country have progressively permitted national radio-television systems to conform to their own country's institutions. Initial dependence in respect to these matrices is visible at all levels. As Rita Cruise O'Brien pointed out in the case of French-speaking Africa:

> When ORTF had been a single state corporation (prior to 1975) it created a service called SOFRATEV, which was established to promote the sale of French equipment to those overseas countries in which ORTF had influence. These activities are now incorporated also in TDF which provides

engineering consultancies to overseas broadcasting systems for feasibility studies and system design. Thomson-France has a monopoly of the material supplied to France's former colonies, which they have purchased extensively since independence (Senegal, for example, was offered a "free trial" run for television for the 1972 Olympic Games which then became the origin of their television system). The equipment provided by any donor in this field is usually tied to home-country manufacturers, and therefore the net result of the French system is probably no different than any other. The surprising aspect is the level of integration of training, technical assistance, and equipment provision in a single organisation, which compared with the other two major donors (Britain and the United States) is exceptional.[47]

In 1972 I analysed the way in which ABC, CBS, NBC and the Time-Life group were intimately linked to the historical trajectory of television systems in Latin American countries. At the time, I wrote:

ABC Worldvision, which has financial interests in the television systems of sixty-three countries, has financial interests in television stations in Guatemala, El Salvador, Honduras, Costa Rica, Panama, Mexico, Colombia, Venezuela, Ecuador, Argentina, and Chile. (In Chile television was first launched by the universities and only later by the state). In 1960 after the creation of the Central American common market, ABC invested in five Central American stations and created CATVN (Central American TV Network), which offered three functions in the same centralised service: program purchasing, sales representations, and the setting up of channels. Early in 1968, ABC repeated this operation in South America by creating along the same lines LATINO (Latin American Television International Network), which according to the *Television Factbook 1968–9*, brings together Channel 9 of Buenos Aires, Channels 13 and 4 from Chile, 9 from Bogota, 7 from Costa Rica, 7 from the Dominican Republic, three Ecuadorian channels, two channels from El Salvador, Channel 5 from Honduras, 6 from Nicaragua, 2 from Panama, 2 from Caracas, 12 from Uruguay, 3 from Guatemala, etc. . . ."[48]

The influence of the American model is such that today only 15 percent of radio and television systems in Latin America are governed by the public sector (compared to 85.1 percent for radio and 92.8 percent for television in Africa, 78 percent for radio in Asia, and 77.4 percent for radio in Europe). The transposition of these models is made in conditions that aggravate their negative aspects. The Venezuelan researcher Antonio Pasquali indicates, in a book published in 1980, "In Venezuela, the broadcast of advertisements reached an average of 1,313 a day, that is, at the time when this evaluation was made, this quota exceeded the North American level for television advertising by 61 percent."[49] We will return to this theme when we talk about the effects on consumption models. When the famous educational series "Sesame Street," developed in the United States on the fringe of the large commercial channels, was adapted and distributed in Latin America, the first image of this noncommercial series bore the credit "Xerox presents." In other words, commercial television becomes a compulsory channel for products developed outside the commercial orbit of the home country.

The dominance of transnational conglomerates in television has its counterpart in other sectors of the cultural industry. Thus, it is impossible to grasp the importance of CBS or RCA-NBC without analysing their share of the world record industry. In Brazil, for example, transnational firms control 75.4 percent of the LP record market and 53.1 percent of the singles market. RCA alone controls 44.5 percent of the LP market. Polygram (owned by Philips and Siemens) controls 20 percent. The other companies present are CBS, EMI, and Warners. In Mexico transnational firms control 53 percent of the singles market (RCA 15.4 percent, CBS 12.7 percent).[50] Is it necessary to add that in these two Latin American countries, RCA, CBS, and Philips have been the pioneers of the electronics industry, and in the case of CBS, the educational and toy industries. The first transnational firms of radio-broadcasting equipment bear their label.

How are the catalogs of these firms in peripheral countries made up? Let us take the case of Brazil, for which we have some available information and which represents a relatively privileged situation in the Third World, as its national music has achieved an international status and prestige. In 1976 EMI launched 143 foreign records against 85 national ones; Warner 48 foreign against 6 national; the national manager of Phonogram, after having carried out a survey, noted in 1976 that the number of national releases increased by 47 percent and that international releases increased by 76 percent. All the directors of these transnational firms justified their preference for imported records on economic grounds, "A national release must sell at least ten thousand copies to cover costs, whereas an international one does so with a sale of five thousand." This disequilibrium between the national and the international has direct repercussions for radio programing and according to the above study, radio programing in large cities is 75 percent foreign music, whereas national music is broadcast above all by radios in the interior of Brazil.[51]

The presence of transnational firms in peripheral countries has not prevented countries like Mexico and Brazil from forming large cultural con-glomerates controlled by the local bourgeoisie, whose relative power in the national territory exceeds that exercised by oligopolies in central countries like the United States or Great Britain. This is the case, for example, of Televisa in Mexico, which concurrently controls four television channels. It has an average of 85 percent of the television audience, a cable television company, a television production center (in 1979 according to its own figures, exports to the United States, Central and South America, the West Indies, and now, to Arab countries, represented 24,000 television hours a year"), an advertising production company, a transmission relay system for the United States in areas where there are large Spanish-speaking concen-trations (Univision), five radio stations, a publishing section that puts out numerous magazines on television, cinema, and women. Its latest creation, profiting from the dismanteling of the state cinema industry, is Televicine, which aims to produce professional feature films. Televisa is also a channel for educational television, has interests in the record industry, and owns several television channels in the United States.

Advertising Network

The transnational network constructed by advertising agencies is almost as old as the cinema network and in some cases even older. Agencies have only followed in the footsteps of transnational firms overseas. J. Walter Thomp-son, one of the world's largest advertising agencies, was already installed in India, Argentina, Brazil, and Uruguay in 1929. In 1979 American trans-nationals occupied thirty of the top fifty places in the advertising industry. Japan followed with two; France, four; Brazil, two; and West Germany and Switzerland, one each. The foreign operations of the top ten U.S. agencies represented 50.4 percent of their gross income. J. Walter Thompson's foreign revenue represented 54 percent of its gross, and that of McCann-Erickson came to 73 percent. J. Walter Thompson is present in twenty-nine countries and McCann-Erickson in fifty-eight. In fact in the peripheral countries, no French, British, or Japanese agency can seriously compete with the overall network of U.S. agencies. Thus, the billings of the UNIVAS network (a Franco-Anglo-American network started up by the French agency, Havas) were $596 million as against $2,964 million earned by the leading world agency, Interpublic Group in 1979.[52] Whereas in developed countries, trans-national agencies gained roughly half the market, in the Caribbean they gained 92 percent of it; in Africa where the invasion has only just started,

83 percent; and in Latin America, 58.2 percent.[53] This is in spite of a climate judged unfavourable by the American advertisers' journal *Advertising Age*. "The one real threat these agencies seem to face abroad, especially in the Third World, where much of the global growth will probably be in the next decade, is being legislated out of a country. Advertising in much of the Third World is considered by government authorities as part of the vital communications sector. Already, India has limited ownership by outside agencies to 40 percent of a domestic shop, while a number of South American countries hold the line of foreign investment to 20 percent."[54]

In effect, it is difficult to establish a typology of modes of penetration of advertising agencies in foreign countries. In Kenya, for example, in 1979 McCann-Erickson acquired the assets of that country's second largest agency, Advertising Associates. McCann-Erikson Worldwide, which established offices in Nairobi in 1975, has now become the largest agency in Kenya. In Nigeria after the enactment of the Nigerian Enterprises Promotion Decree, all equity in advertising agencies is held by Nigerian nationals only. However, as *Advertising Age* makes clear, "Affiliate status with the parent agency is ensured by one means or another."[55] Among the ten biggest agencies in Nigeria, the largest consumer of advertising in Africa after South Africa, the three biggest are American: Lintas Nigeria (part of the Interpublic group like McCann-Erickson); Ogilvy, Benson and Mather; and Grant Advertising (an affiliate of McCann-Erickson). Invariably the same advertisers reappear: in Nigeria companies of the Unilever group constitute by themselves close to 40 percent of all advertising expenditure, and Beecham make up 20 percent. In Latin America where the relations of force vary widely from country to country, several agencies like Leo Burnett and BBDO (Batten, Barton, Durstine and Osborne) announced in 1979 that they were in the process of acquiring new subsidiaries in Argentina, whereas in the Andean pact countries, other American agencies announced that they were in the process of affiliating themselves to national agencies following a ruling limiting ownership of advertising agencies. However, in other countries like Mexico, direct control is still acceptable. "The US influence on the Mexican advertising scene is still very much alive . . . ownership is still largely retained in the US. Of the 15 agencies that handle about 75 percent of the country's total advertising billings, only 5 are wholly Mexican-owned."[56]

Invariably firms found at the head of the list of advertisers are for the most part transnational; 80.3 percent of the advertising space of the Colombian version of the womens' magazine, *Cosmopolitan*; 75.5 percent of the Venezuelan version; and 73.7 percent of the Mexican version are taken up by transnational advertising.[57] The advertising investments of transnational firms operate in Latin America in strict liason with the commercial radio-television system, following lines completely different from those of developed countries. Witness, for example, the case of advertising on Venezuelan television mentioned earlier. According to a technical report by the United Nations Center on Transnational Corporations, a comparison of advertising expenditure by media category throughout the world reveals that print is still the most important means with 43 percent of the return (study carried out in ninety-six countries in 1976). Television came in second place with 21 percent, and radio third with 7 percent. In Western Europe and the United States and Canada, television received 14 percent and 20 percent of the takings respectively. In Latin America television attained 41 percent.[58] This percentage, however, is easily exceeded in Mexico where television absorbs 62 percent of advertising expenses. Commented a Mexican researcher: "In 1976 Mexico occupied sixty-fourth place in terms of gross national product per capita; that same year, however, Mexico occupied eighth place in terms of television advertising. Only the United States, Japan, Great Britain, Brazil, Canada, West Germany, and Austria spent more in absolute terms on television advertising."[59] These statistics are only mentioned to suggest the intimate relation existing between a communication system and an advertising network.

The transnational advertising network is also an education network:

> Certainly one of the greatest contributions made by American advertising agencies has been their role as training centers for the ad communities around the globe. A Danish advertising man commented to *Advertising Age* last year that in the '50s when marketing as a conscious skill was dawning in Europe, those who knew the basics "were the real winners," and generally speaking, that meant Unilever-trained managers and middle managers. They were the ones that scored the points and stood out from the rest. In Mexico, Colgate-Palmolive, P and G, GF, Anderson Clayton, and Richardson-Merril have filled the role of educator. Virtually every agency has at least one marketing man who was skilled in one of the American MNs. "Colgate, particularly, is constantly feeding our industry with people," say Augusto Elias, head of the Publicidad Augusto Elias agency. On the agency side, many of today's Mexican agency owners came out of the executive ranks of Chicago's now-defunct Grant Advertising agency.[60]

Finally, it must be pointed out that the degree of internationalization that can be found in the advertising industry can also be found in many other branches of the service industries, with the same predominance of American firms. There are few peripheral countries that have never had to do business with the Big Eight U.S. accounting firms, whose overseas earnings reached 47 percent in 1978; or with research companies like A.C. Nielsen, which alone earned almost half the revenue of the top ten American research firms with 45 percent of its earnings from foreign countries; or, yet again, with IMS International, which has specialised in the transnational promotion of pharmaceutical products, drawing 60 percent of their 1977 earnings from foreign countries.[61]

Publishing Network

The first published products to be massively dumped onto the international market have been comics. Celebrating the fiftieth anniversary in September 1980 of "Blondie," one of its numerous comic characters, the King Features Syndicate, owned by the Hearst newspaper group, recalled that "Blondie" had been translated into fifteen languages, sold to eighteen hundred newspapers and was read daily by 150 million readers in fifty-five countries.[62] This example is typical of the internationalization of the circulation of these products, conceived principally for children but also for adults. Through this internationalization Walt Disney productions will not only have the right to more translations but also unlimited expansion through games, films, television programs, amusement parks, and so forth, to such an extent that when it becomes a question of finding an alternative to Disney products in childrens' films, for example, the Disney model will be so naturalized, internationalized, that there will be no opening whatsoever. Other transnational firms, like Bobbs-Merril, the educational division of ITT, producer of an alternative type of childrens' film (*Raggedy Ann* and *Raggedy Andy*) learned to their expense in 1977 that the collective memory forged since 1930 in generations of children (and adults) in both the developed and peripheral worlds, by "Disneyan taste," was a force to be reckoned with. In Paris a director as famous as the Italian, Comencini, with his own version of *Pinocchio,* had to be content with a single cinema attracting 47,200 spectators in forty-seven weeks, whereas Disney's *Pinocchio* attracted ten times as many spectators in ten weeks. There are very few studies specifying the vulnerability of the childrens' sector to transnational products. However, here and there we can find information allowing a deeper analysis. Under the title, "Childrens' books: denationalization is their favourite dish," the Brazilian sociologist R. A. Amaral noted:

"The denationalization tendency reaches a peak in childrens' literature where an overwhelming majority of the titles and products are foreign. The text, the illustrations, the paper, the printing, the cover, and the finishing are all foreign. . . . Here is an example. The bookshop at Galeao airport in Rio de Janeiro, known for the variety of publications offered, had 153 childrens' titles available on July 11, 1976. Of these, barely 13 were printed in Brazil from foreign plates; 118 were written, composed, printed, and bound overseas, mainly in Japan, Spain, and England. Of the 153 books, only 5 were written by a Brazilian author and produced in Brazil. As for the comic books, out of 174 titles, only 2 were Brazilian, *Monica* and *Cebolinha*, written by Mauricio de Souza."[63]

After comics, whose internationalization goes back to before the Second World War, it was the turn of products like *Readers Digest, Time,* and *Life* to penetrate the exterior market, principally in Latin America, on the occasion of the struggle against the fascist Axis powers. Today *Reader's Digest* is published in fourteen languages, forty-one editions and is sold in more than a hundred countries.

One had to wait for the great wave of transnationalization of the world economy in the 1960s and 1970s to see the internationalization of a train of publications up until then reserved for an American clientele. This accounts for the success of the Hearst group that today publishes editions of *Popular Mechanics, Good Housekeeping,* and *Cosmopolitan* in Spanish, French, Portuguese, and other languages, without counting its numerous popular almanacs. Business magazines, privileged carriers of business culture, covering all sectors of professional activity from engineering to architecture and aeronautics, follow in the same path. The most renowned representative is undoubtedly the American firm, McGraw-Hill, with sixty-one magazines, newsletters and newswires. Today its magazine *Business Week* counts over 5.5 million readers. According to the magazine's own publicity: "You know that today, more and more businesses see the world as a single market. Business knows no borders. And business leaders everywhere share a whole world of common needs. Not the least of these is *Business Week* worldwide, which now offers global marketers a more efficient, more flexible way to reach business leaders everywhere." To give but one other example, *Aviation Week and Space Technology,* which had a print run of more than a 100 thousand copies and over 500 thousand readers in 129 countries, who were, for the most part, executives, officers, and scientists within the aeronautic industry and the airforces. In a study undertaken by UNESCO, four German researchers analysed the internationalization of this type of journal and its role in the advertising and public relations areas of the arms industry.[64] In other words, very few professional domains remain on the fringe of the internationalization process. How could it be otherwise, when we know that the first journals to be internationalized, at the same time as the *Readers' Digest,* were journals of the American army like *Military Review,* which, from the 1940s, on, were published in Spanish and Portuguese editions for the subcontinent?

The internationalization strategies for these products are far from being uniform.[65] Some transnational companies prefer to principally retain the English language, for example, rather than translate or adapt into other languages. This is not only the case of news magazines like *Time* and *Newsweek,* but also that of the majority of McGraw-Hill's professional magazines. (the only parts likely to be modified according to the countries in which they are sold are the advertisements, as is the case in *Business Week*). This is not the case, however, in the *Reader's Digest,* as one of its directors recalled in 1979, "Unlike *Time,* which calls itself international, though published in only one language, we prefer to describe ourselves as a national magazine in a large number of countries."[66] But even if one seeks to declare oneself national by publishing in the language of a country, there are numerous ways this can be done. Some like the Hearst corporation, prefer a franchise administration: "With the exception of England, where it wholly owns about ten magazines, Hearst licenses about 35 foreign editors through a royalty arrangement, a clean, easy, non-controversial way to work. Hearst skims off a percentage of net revenue and leaves the local operation entirely up to the licensee."[67] This strategy is justified because, "in Brazil, it must come over as an Brazilian magazine, not as a warmed-over American version." As for McGraw-Hill, which owns the entire control for all overseas subsidiaries, it has taken a different route with its foreign-published magazines, maintaining a 49/51 ownership.[68] *Reader's Digest*—which is more than the publication of a magazine as it is also the owner of book-clubs, records and sales by correspondence—maintains that "the magazine is self-sufficient in each country, with its own editor and editorial content. Editors can draw upon US material and adapt it for their own country and occasionally there is a world release of one significant article which appears almost simultaneously in all editions."[69] This claim is completely relative since not so long ago, Canada, for example, required 80 percent of the editorial content of various U.S. magazines like the *Reader's Digest* to be different from that of the parent publication. The latest example is *Scientific American,* the most recent entry onto the international market. In the five versions that it publishes (Italian,

Spanish, French, Japanese, and German), seven out of eight articles come from the United States. *Scientific American* maintains 50/50 joint stock ventures whereby "we furnish the editorial and our partner runs the business."[70]

The transnational magazine publishing network is largely dominated by American firms. In the book sector, on the other hand, one finds most of the old colonial powers. The French publishing house, Hachette, for example, has offices in Tunisia, Morocco, Senegal, the Ivory Coast, Gabon, Cameroon, the Congo, Zaire, and many other former French colonies. It is also in Brazil, Argentina, Lebanon, and Egypt.[71] English firms like Longmans, a company that dates back 250 years, took 80 percent of its turnover in 1972 from overseas. Its network of branches extends from Hong Kong to the Caribbean, taking in South Africa, East and West Africa, all the Arab world, as well as Malaysia, Singapore, Australia, and New Zealand. Longmans is one of many companies of the Pearson publishing empire, which owns, among other concerns, the *Financial Times* and Penguin Books.

German companies like Bertelsmann do not lag behind, since this firm is associated with, for example, the largest publishing group in Brazil (Abril) in the *Circulo do livro,* "the largest book club in Latin America and the best channel so far devised to cope with Brazil's inadequate retail infrastructure."[72] The majority of large American firms, particularly those that publish scholarly, technical, and scientific works like John Wiley and Sons have numerous contacts in Third World countries where they generally have a great deal of influence in higher education. Other firms like McGraw-Hill do not limit themselves to this higher level. According to the world publishing directory, already in 1970 for the Far East market they published in Singapore and Kuala Lumpur textbooks for primary, secondary, and technical teaching in several national languages of the region. In India in conjunction with the local group Tata they published these same textbooks in various Indian languages. Opening a branch in Panama at the same time, they undertook the translation of American textbooks into Spanish for Spanish America; in Brazil they even managed to make their textbooks compulsory for all levels of teaching, thanks to an agreement with the Ministry of Education in 1967.[73] In fact, McGraw-Hill is now involved in publishing books and magazines in eighteen different countries and ten different languages.

The importance of the transnational book network is obviously extremely different according to the country involved. It reaches a peak in the African countries. Demonstrating how African countries continue to be dependant on the Western model for television as well as for radio, the British sociologist Peter Golding wrote:

Similarly in publishing, state publishing establishments have very often relied on British or American publishing and commercial expertise. The most familiar example is that of Anglophone Africa. Macmillan and Co. organised arrangements with governments in Ghana, Uganda, Zambia, Tanzania and Nigeria during the 1960s, which eventually became state publishing houses. As in broadcasting, the legacy of the initial coupling is often a permanent relationship. As Nottingham puts it, "Outside interests get much of their profits from producing the material concerned from outside Africa and selling it to these [state] publishing houses which become mere merchandising depots."[74]

Challenging the publishing policy of transnational firms in the English-speaking countries of Central Africa, another researcher noted:

The multinational publishers do not have a function fundamentally different from the one they exercise at home; namely to publish works destined for a classical type of teaching that has the effect of reinforcing the idea that books are synonymous with education to the detriment of extra-curricular education and the simple pleasure of reading. Thus, there has hardly been any investment in complementary texts to teach literacy and books for young people, even though such works play a vital role in the growth of reading habits and therefore the enlargement and development of the book market. The multinationals have neglected literacy-teaching materials and books for children because illiteracy and linguistic fragmentation make for small print runs and insignificant profits as the buying power of potential readers is weak or nonexistent and, in part, because they are essentially concerned with educational works of the classic type and prestige publications that only serve short-term interests of elites and multinational publishers.[75]

With examples like the purchase of a regional satellite in Latin America and Brazil that we mentioned previously, and those we have just mentioned concerning educational texts, we now have two serious axes of reflection on the penetration of transnational firms into the formal education systems of peripheral countries. It must be mentioned, however, that because the education system is integrated into the state apparatus, it presents more contradictions and therefore greater resistance to norms of transnationalization. The logic pressing the formal education system to meet up with mass culture in the expansion of capital will only step up the challenge. However, transnational culture has not waited for this moment to stream into the classroom. At the beginning of the school year in August 1980 in Mexico, a journalist made a count of the number of educational supplies through which a young Mexican pupil could encounter the transnational world: Kimberley Clark, with its notebooks, transported children in Ford cars to sunny tourist beaches and lakes; Samsonite boasted of schoolcases, pencil cases and brief cases; Wereaver launched a new ball point pen. The greatest novelty of the season— globes from Chicago.[76]

News Agencies

This is the sector of the information industry best known to the public, for it is from this sector that the nonaligned countries, have since 1975 contested the way in which transnational firms conceive of culture and information. Four large agencies dominate the market: UPI, AP, Reuters, and AFP. During the debates on what has now been dubbed the new international information order, exhibits for the prosecution were in abundance.

A study undertaken in 1975 in Latin America on the majority of the important newspapers of the subcontinent showed that 39 percent of the international news reproduced in the newspapers of large cities came from UPI, 21 percent from AP, 10 percent from AFP, 9 percent from Reuter Latin, 8 percent from EFE (a Spanish agency), 4 percent from Latin (the agency partly controled by certain Latin American newspapers), and 0.3 percent from Prensa Latina, the Cuban press agency. According to this study, the two large American agencies therefore supplied 50 percent of the international information published daily in Latin America. However, a similar study in 1962 revealed an 80 percent dependence on the two large American news agencies. This swing has worked out in favour of large American newspapers like the *New York Times* or the *Washington Post* or French newspapers like *Le Monde* which increasingly distribute pre-prepared editorials. As for images and graphic materials, the great majority (nearly 90 percent) of international telephotos reproduced in Latin American newspapers came exclusively from AP and UPI.[77]

As the Tunisian Minister of Information pointed out:

> The disequilibrium is flagrant and even worrying. Almost 80 percent of the news circulating in the world comes from international or transnational agencies. Unfortunately, these agencies only devote 20 to 30 percent of this news to developing countries that, nevertheless, represent, almost three-quarters of humanity. The five largest international news agencies alone monopolize the essential of human and material potential.

They group together over five hundred offices and support 4,319 overseas correspondents or free-lancers in 116 countries; every day on average they diffuse between 15 and 17 million words, whereas nearly a third of developing countries do not even have their own national news agency. This disequilibrium also reigns over the distribution of the spectrum of radio frequencies. Developed countries hold nearly 90 percent of the source of this spectrum . . . [78]

In terms of adaptation strategies, recent indications show that in those continents where the pressure is now too great to continue with the old ground rules, American agencies or at least one of them, are attempting to associate with local press groups. Thus, in July 1980 in Miami the first meeting of the Junta Assesora Latinoamericana of UPI took place. This association presents itself as the first newspaper association outside of the United States to meet on a regular basis to help UPI adapt to their needs. Among the members of its Board are the directors of *El Universal* (Mexico), *Listin Diario* (Dominican Republic), *Panorama* (Maracaibo, Venezuela), *El Tiempo* (Bogota), and *El Universo* (Guayaquil). Also present at this meeting were representatives of *O Globo* (Rio de Janeiro) and *La Tercera de la Hora* (Chile). [79]

The same type of operation, aimed at local groups, has already been seen in the domain of advertising agencies where Crain Communication (the publisher of *Advertising Age,* the weekly bible of advertising executives the world over), after having started up a similar group the preceeding year to link up Europeans, announced in 1979 the formation of the Latin America advisory council: "The council, headed by Richard B. Criswell of Leo Burnett in Chicago, will serve as a sounding board on major advertising and marketing issues affecting Latin America."[80] All the Latin American countries are represented through the directors of the large advertising agencies. The marketing directors of large transnational firms like Johnson and Johnson, Nestlé, and Gerber are sometimes also represented.

Linguistic Network

As we have already seen, business and news magazines of American origin have a strategy of international penetration using the English language. Given their target, this is the best way of reaching their so-called international audience. As *Newsweek* indicated in January 1973 at the launching of their new international edition: "We have introduced the first *truly* international news magazine, a news magazine whose minds are as international as its readers." *Newsweek* specified its definition of "international minds" as "the men who make the decisions in the business world and the political leaders of all the world's nations."[81] These are only some of many indications that show that English is on the way to becoming (some would say already comfortably installed as) the only currency of international exchange, the *lingua franca* of commerce, science, and technology.

Above all, English is the language that managers of the large transnational firms must speak. The linguistic policy of transnational firms is constructed on the hegemony of English, or rather Anglo-American. As the French linguist, Henri Gobard, points out, this is not the English of Shakespeare but of Berlitz. Karl Sauvant argues:

> Managers of United States and British affiliates abroad—which account for about two thirds of all foreign affiliates—have always had to report to their headquarters in English. It seems, however, that non-Anglo-American enterprises can not escape this trend: several Swedish multinationals, among them SKF, have adopted English as the official company language for all international publications, charts, manuals, head office announcements and all correspondance involving more than one affiliate; Nestlé uses French and English as the enterprise's two languages. Finally, Philips have gone so far as to adopt English for all their internal correspondance.[82]

English is also the principal language for the teaching of management, serving as the language of communication between the students and trainees of the management schools founded by large transnational firms. It is, for example, the language that must be spoken by the African manager sent to Management Center Europe in Brussels (an offshoot of the American Management Association) or to the Foundation for Business Administration in Rotterdam, set up by Unilever, Akzo, Shell, and so forth unless he is lucky enough to be sent to the Institut Européen d'Administration des Affaires (INSEAD) in Fontainebleau or the Centre d'Education Permanente (CEDEP), founded by one of the biggest perfume and cosmetic multinationals, L'Oreal (which bought both the Marie-Claire Album firm that publishes four large-circulation women's magazines and Interedit, which publishes the French version of *Cosmopolitan* in 1967). These latter two training centers are bilingual, even though the method of teaching management is one and the same. A report of the Chemical Bank, though recognizing the rivalry between the prestigious state-run French *grandes écoles* and business schools, asserted, "Even traditional university-affiliated business faculties such as the one at the Catholic University of Louvain (Belgium) or the prestigious Ecole des Hautes Etudes Commerciales in Paris have introduced U.S. teaching methods, which are characterised by the use of the Harvard-pioneered approach for teaching management skills."[83] The penetration of transnational norms in university faculties of commerce and economics in peripheral countries is not an isolated, exclusive phenomenon. And when transnational instructors do not speak the language of the country, the language of technology fills the gap. In the January 21, 1980, edition of *Computer World,* one reads: "Santiago, Chile. Latin American students enrolled in a Pertec Computer Corp. (PCC) training session here discovered recently that language is never a barrier as long as the language is DP (Data Processing). Although the Pertec instructor spoke no Spanish and the 15 students enrolled in the course didn't speak English, communication was established through the languages of Basic and Cobol, according to Ed Towers, regional sales manager of PCC's Latin American Operations."[84]

This irony, however, is out of place, as the accepted language of international computer technology is also English. As a report by a consultant firm for the U.S. Department of Commerce on the Venezuelan market for computers and related equipment recalled: "Few of the companies in the market give good personal training, printed matter in Spanish is often deficient or non-existent, software support is generally poor and non-competitive with software houses. U.S. manufacturers must guard against a determined foreign competitor making use of these evident weaknesses."[85]

To understand the extent of this shortcoming, it needs to be specified that Venezuela does not have its own computer industry. All computers and related equipment are imported. American firms, from the factories in the United States or through their mainly Brazilian subsidiaries, control between 90 and 95 percent of the Venezuelan market. The development of computerization has been so rapid over the last three years that the above-mentioned report remarked that "the technology time lag between the U.S. and Venezuela has shortened considerably. New systems are often introduced here within one year of their commercial baptism at home." The reaction of transnational firms to the decision of the French government to no longer accept the circulation of products with directions in English is indicative of a widespread feeling: "These manufacturers argue that they simply do not have the facilities to translate the enormous body of documentation that accompanies their products, and that in any event such a translation would be prohibitively costly and time-consuming. The language of most high-technology fields, they point out, is English and specialists, wherever they are, are taught from standard American texts and manuals."[86]

English is also the language of science. As the President of the twenty-fifth Congress of the American Association of Information Science asserted: "The construction of international networks takes place through the recognition of English. . . . The acceptance of English as *the* international language constitutes a decisive step towards the internationalization of information networks."[87] It is from Europe that the most virulent protests have recently arisen against these pretensions that affect both pure and applied sciences. In the question of language the question of the domination of data banks by American firms can also be found; 70 percent of data banks are American and practically all transatlantic links are controlled by American firms, IBM and RCA enjoying the dominant position. Large American information feeders like Lockheed already realize at least 20 percent of their turnover in Europe. Certain sectors of information, particularly chemical information, are an American monopoly to such an extent that resistance, in some people's eyes, is futile. This monopoly, in turn, reinforces the position of English as the language of scientific exchange, publication, and commercial exchange. This phenomenon has been studied by a French scientist who has clearly shown how one monopoly reinforces another, casting national researchers out into the circuit of international publications, that is, the circuit of publications in English.

> The fact that the major portion of the world's literature on chemistry is in English can be attributed to three main reasons. The first is the employment of English as the national language in many countries. The second is that many scientists, living in countries with a little-known language, prefer to publish their articles directly in English. The Chemical Abstract Service (CAS), the American monopoly over chemical information, lies behind the third reason. In effect, CAS is equipped solely to help those who understand English. The de facto acceptance of English as the language of chemical documentation reinforces still more the American monopoly in this field. The introduction of data written solely in English in systems like MEDLARS or CAS induces scientists to publish in English-language journals. It is a vicious circle; to be read, one must be known, and to be known, it is advisable to be cited in *Current Contents*, CAS, or in other secondary American publications corresponding to the appropriate domain."[88]

A study carried out in Europe in 1977 on documentary systems and networks indicated that in 337 centres of bibliographical data using computers, 10 used German, 10 used French, 76 used English, whereas 4 were in other languages (Russian, Japanese, Swedish) or were multilingual. Of 149 data banks, more than 66 used English.[89] Other French scientists have shown that American domination over data banks bears some relation to the decline of national medical and scientific journals. In 1980 the scientific community saw the internationalization of three large American scientific journals (*Journal of the American Medical Association, The Medical Letter,* and *Scientific American*). For their part, some scientific publishing houses increasingly resented the need to link up with American firms to cover and penetrate the international market.[90] In 1977 Editions Doin, one of the pillars of French medical publishing since 1874, were taken over by Saunders, a division of the conglomerate CBS. To obtain the permission of the French government, CBS committed itself "to maintain and develop the French company's domestic list and it is expected that this arrangement will also help obtain an international audience for Doin's own authors." CBS, however, added that it would "emphasise translation into French of English scientific and medical texts."[91]

These transformations, which are taking place on the brink of the information era, have already been analysed in some peripheral countries like Brazil. At the world conference on policies of transborder data flow, the Brazilian delegate emphasised that countries that did not concern themselves with the control of strategic information resources risked becoming intolerably dependent in the telecommunications field on foreign political and economic interest groups. He spoke in veiled terms against American and European transnationals and insisted that "the information industry threatens cultural identity as automatized information carries with it the culture of those who produce it."[92]

Tourist Network

I am only going to briefly discuss this source of transnational values since we will be returning to this question in other sections. It will be sufficient to indicate the transnational character of the tourist industry, based on studies by the United Nations Center on Transnational Corporations. At the end of 1978, 81 transnational hotel corporations were active in the world hotel industry—72 from developed market economies and 9 from developing countries. These 81 corporations were associated with 1,025 hotels outside the home country with a total of 270,646 rooms. This was equivalent to 18.5 percent of the estimated total domestic and foreign rooms of the 100 largest and leading smaller hotel chains. This is the best available assessment of the transnational nature of worldwide hotel industry.

There are four major categories of transnational hotel: hotel chains connected with airlines (16 transnational corporations); hotel chains connected with tour operators (six); management advisory companies (three); and independent hotel chains—that is, hotels not associated with any other tourist-related body. Transnational-associate hotels abroad are generally classified as four or five-star quality and tend to be larger than indigenous hotels.

Transnational corporations based in the United States account for nearly 50 percent of the transnational-associate hotels abroad and 56 each account for about 15 percent of the associate hotels abroad and about 12 percent of the rooms. The remaining hotels abroad are associated with transnationals from seventeen other countries, including five developing countries. Transnational hotels based in those five developing countries account for about 4 percent of both the transnational-associate hotels abroad and rooms in those hotels.[93]

To indicate the degree of normative centralization of one of the components of the tourist industry chain, we only have to note that, in general, international hotel and catering chains acquire only 10 to 30 percent of their equipment (furniture and carpeting, kitchen equipment, building supplies for remodeling, china, glassware and silver) from the area in which they are installed. Thus, for the Inter-Continental (Hilton's), 40 percent of its food, 80 percent of its linen, 75 percent of its paper and disposable products, and 100 percent of its audiovisual, discotheque, and meeting room equipment are bought by the Head Office. "Not that this means all products are purchased from U.S. suppliers, but rather that the top executive office maintains a tight reign."[94]

A final remark before closing this overview of transnational culture networks. Many of the central and marginal annotations throughout this analysis have tried to suggest the differential degree of exposure to transnational commodities. All countries are not subjected in the same way to these networks. The more they are incorporated into the transnational economic system, the more they are subjected. In black Africa, where the arrival of transnational advertising agencies was an important component in the conformation of its communication system, few countries (apart from Nigeria) can compete with the structure of "transnational modernity" displayed by the majority of Latin American countries. Let us remember that 45 percent of developing countries are still without television. We must therefore be wary of the myth of the "global village," which is far from being a reality in many countries and regions. Although their standard of living is roughly the same, Andean Indians and Southern African peasants can be very differently exposed to the benefits and ravages of transnational culture.

Some groups more than others are subjected to transnational circuits. There is no need to draw up a transnational flow diagram to realize that managers are subjected to an overdose, as much in their work as in their leisure or training. The "middle classes," a generic category that the transnationals themselves define in terms of the role this social strata plays in the central countries, particularly in the United States, are the classes that after managers dispose of the biggest range of possibilities of contact with transnational products. A large portion of transnational publications are aimed at them. As proof of this, we only have to consult the transnationals' own profile of their clientele: "*Reader's Digest* readers are educated, 'far from poor,' family-oriented, involved in the world about them and 'concerned about the future, perhaps with a tinge of nostalgia for simpler days.' "[95] *Geografía Universal,* the Mexican version of *National Geographic,* indicated for its part that "about 82% of the 275,000 readers are in the upper-middle class or higher, according to a survey conducted by the Mexican affiliate of Gallup International Research: 47% are company owners, presidents, administrators or managers, while 20% are doctors, lawyers, engineers etc. . . . Another 64% own their own houses."[96] *Buenhogar,* the Spanish American version of *Good Housekeeping,* defines its readers, exact copies of their American counterparts, thus: "Our publication is addressed to the modern Latin American young woman, of good education, married and well off. Her interests are no different from those of her North American counterpart."[97]

In the world of publishing, the "working-class transnational" *(transnational populaire)* only seems to exist for women and children. The former, in Latin America, are exposed to transnational firms of a particular type such as the group Bloque de Armas which, from Miami, have not only internationalized the magazines of the Hearst group but have also unloaded millions of copies of *fotonovelas* aimed at working-class women. Comics, on the other hand, are read by children of all social classes. This shows once again that women and children are particularly suitable generic categories for facilitating the penetration of transnational products. "Women are the same the whole world over," advertisers love to say. As the firm Helena Rubenstein put it: "The differences are in the degree of sophistication of distribution and marketing, not in the women. . . . In some areas of Latin America, women have simply not been exposed to as many products, but potential heavy users of cosmetics exist everywhere and will respond to the same promise of beauty."[98]

Even if, in their everyday lives, the popular strata are constantly in contact with multiple signs of transnationality (supermarkets, advertising billboards, the street itself), they also have the most one dimensional contact with audiovisual media. A study undertaken in 1972–73 in Santiago, Chile, by Michèle Mattelart and Mabel Piccini showed that "deprived of other sources of formal and informal education and recreation, the popular classes are only too anxious to obtain the maximum profit from television as a source of culture. As a woman from a shantytown said, 'People from rich suburbs have other ways of amusing themselves and don't attach much importance to television. It is very important for us however.' Another resident added: 'Comrades make sacrifices to buy TV sets; and afterwards, they naturally want to profit the maximum from them. Every evening they are glued to their television sets and watch everything.' "[99]

Sociocultural Investments

What definitive values, modes of behavior, aspirations, and model of society does the structure of transnational transmission carry?

Let us hear the directors of transnational firms or media. Interviewed in 1972 by *U.S. News and World Report,* a former executive of CBS, who had become a director of the USIS (U.S. Information Service) before returning to the private sector as the director of the educational television division of Westinghouse, declared: "The whole communications revolution was created by the United States. The technology which is the essence of the communications revolution was created in this country. In the use of that technology for the dissemination of ideas and information and entertainment, we were the world's leaders. We dominated motion pictures and television for years. We still do. 'Madison Avenue' has become a world wide cliché for referring to the technique of marketing, and that's the dissemination of ideas."[100]

In 1974 David Olgivy, founder of one of the largest transnational advertising agencies, wrote: "Thus, *Digest* readers have a profound influence on people who are free to read what they want. *This magazine exports the best in American life.* In my opinion, the Digest is doing as much as the United States Information Agency to win the battle for men's minds."[101] In 1979, commenting on the large growth of transnational advertising networks, an analyst wrote in *Advertising Age:* "It could be said that advertising and marketing can be a nation's unofficial diplomat overseas, representing a country's way of life more dramatically and realistically than official state department or foreign office ambassadors. The tremendous international impact of marketing and advertising in the United States, in fact, led to the coining of the word 'adplomacy.' "[102]

Finally in 1977–78, celebrating the unprecedented success of "hamburger bars," "coffee shops," "fish and chip shops," and "donut bars" in the Far East, where the fast-food multinational, McDonalds, has had enormous success, *Business Week* exclaimed: "The Americanization of the Japanese, in full swing since the occupation, has reached a new peak. Fast foods are becoming a way of life;"[103] and *Advertising Age,* "It is the food of the jeans generation, the new people who are looking to a common culture. South-East Asians of a generation ago thrived on Coca-Colanisation. Now their children are in the middle of the hamburger happening."[104]

These definitions express the profound conviction in numerous transnational circles that the "international life-style" takes as its reference point the "American way of life." This seems to conform to the argument of Marx, who, in referring to the England of last century, wrote: "The most industrialized country presents to other countries the image of their future."

The transnational cultural model corresponds to a style of development that has its instigators, its beneficiary classes, nonbeneficiary classes, its definition of value and of priorities in the use of a country's or group's resources. It is this style of development that structures the messages of transnational agents and is the source of inspiration for their content. It is found as much in the form of conceiving of social relations internal to the transnational firm itself as in the conception of the product and in the relation of networks that the transnational firm weaves with the rest of the outside world.

The Corporation as Sociocultural Investment

The first element of the life-style proposed by the transnational firm, its initial sociocultural investment, is the transnational firm itself. In order to judge the latter as a producer of culture, that is, as a producer of models of social relations between individuals, representations, attitudes and behavior, two different approaches can be adopted. The first consists in seeing how the transnational enterprise conceives of its own system of communication: this is the approach adopted by the specialists of Business and Professional Communication who argue: "Communication is the life blood of the organisation and the means by which management gets things done. The greater emphasis on worldwide competition, depletion of natural resources, social inequities, pollution, and government control points to still greater importance for business to communicate more effectively with all its publics in the future."[105]

One can thus determine the needs of a transnational's members and examine the extent to which they are satisfied. To use the hierarchy of human needs established by the American psychologist Abraham Maslow: physiology, security, acceptance, recognition, and self-actualization. The self-actualized individual "has the feeling that all of his human desires are basically satisfied and that he has reached that place in life in which he finds almost total satisfaction of having achieved what his life's aim has been."[106] From a functionalist perspective, one can very well conclude that from this point of view the Japanese transnational offers far more satisfying communication strategies than North American firms. To quote a passage from a study of this type:

> In the first place all conferences with Japanese firms revealed that executives are very much aware of these basic needs in human beings. Hidehara Takemoto, General Manager of Personnel in the Canon Co. Inc.,—one of the world's leaders of photographic and photocopier equipment—made the following comment, "We have periodic interaction with our university experts so that we can be current, not only on scientific advancement, but also on the latest developments in research that relate to the human being." In all interviews it was found that the interplay between higher education and business is significant. Business knows what the universities are doing and the universities know what is taking place in business. Employees are aware of this interplay, and university professors often lecture to employees on personal well-being, the employees' importance to Japan in the job they are doing, the importance of belonging to their particular company and doing their job better, and, in turn, he points out that this brings fulfillment to their lives [self-actualization]. It is not difficult for the university professor, who is paid from five hundred to one thousand dollars per day for his services, to find the incentive to enhance the prestige of the company to the employees, which heightens the satisfaction of the employees' need for security, affiliation and esteem. The Japanese firm is constantly finding programs to give a strong company image of how the company is working for the best interests of the employees. At this juncture an example will serve to illustrate. When there is a cut in salary, the cut always starts with the top executive and then reaches to the laborer. When there is a raise in salary, the raise always starts with the laborer and proceeds

to management. (Of course the amount of the cut or raise to management is seldom public knowledge). Note, in this feature alone, the tremendous appeal to the spectrum of human needs. It must be readily recognised that these basic needs have a degree of overlap when they are being satisfied, but each need must be satisfied by specific motivational stimulae [sic] in order that a person may experience eventual self-actualisation. It was a revelation to this observer to note the subliminal communication directed to satisfy the human psychological needs which motivates the Japanese worker and, in turn, becomes the single-most force [sic] in the success of the Japanese economy.[107]

Another more critical approach consists in probing transnationals as if they were a system of power. This line of reasoning has been followed for more than three years by four French researchers in an analysis of what they call a "hypermodern corporation." As they were unable to reveal its name, they baptized this firm, one of the biggest transnationals in the information industry, TLTX. These researchers envisage power as a system inscribed within a quadruple coordinate register made up of the economic, the political, the ideological, and the psychological. They reveal the other face of this "brave new world."[108]

Throughout their study, it is, in fact, the mechanisms of "submission to authority" that is studied. This term comes from Stanley Milgram, professor of experimental psychology at Yale University, who was one of the first to have analysed the extreme propensity of adults to submit almost unconditionally to the orders of authority. In the French study, the emphasis was on how individuals submit to the demands of the organization to which they belong, not only through a system of constraints and the fear of repression but also the way in which they interiorize these demands and thus become the subject of their own subjection. Adherence to a system of power is thus internalized.

To outline some of the conclusions of this voluminous piece of research: The specific characteristic of the hypermodern corporation and of neo-capitalist society is the spectacular extension of the power of the economic sphere into the political, ideological and psychological spheres. On the political level, this is shown by the systematic implementation of the techniques of government by remote control: government by regulations replacing personal command, controled autonomy, the centralization-decentralization dialectic (increased decentralization operating within the framework of an enhanced centralization at the level of rules and strategies). At the ideological level, it is shown by the development of a corporation ideology with external and internal use and of ideological practices that reinforce it, notably in the domain of staff policies. On the psychological level, it is evidenced by the orchestration of a number of ways of favoring identification with the organisation and the interiorization of its objectives and values.

These French researchers have analyzed the psychological domination of the organization over the individual, the means by which it acts on the individual unconscious and restructures the defense mechanisms of the individual. The organization acts at one and the same time as an anxiety machine (through its objective power, the position of dependence of the individual to it, and its system of omnipresent control) and as a pleasure machine. It offers different types of pleasure, primarily sado-masochistic (conquest of markets, promotion over others, victory over oneself in the pursuit of an inaccessible ideal) in conformance with its logic, protecting the individual against the anxiety it creates elsewhere. The predominant structure of the unconscious is no longer the relationship to the father, but a maternal form of dependence: identification with the organization has replaced personal identification with the classic corporation head. This is a veritable socio-mental system in which the policies of the organization and the unconscious structures of the individual closely overlap. This involves a dual consequence: on the one hand, the organization produces the individual (who becomes the principal product of the organization, even before the market product) and the individual reproduces the organization by adhering to it in a more perfect way than in the classic organization. On the other hand, the economic and political contradictions of the organization are almost entirely transferred to the level of the individual, who experiences his or her relation to the organization in a contradictory fashion that is at once a source of satisfaction and a prison, an obstacle to self-realisation.

The system of power of the organization is a dialectical system of the mediation of contradictions. Through its system of power, the organization anticipates and mediates the contradictions caused by transformations of the mode of production. In particular, the enhanced role of intellectual work in production requires new forms of cooperation between workers. It demands at the same time, new forms of control to subordinate workers, cooperating in the process of transformed production, to capitalist objectives of profit, world conquest, and expansion. New power structures respond both to this dual objective and to this contradiction. By increasingly integrating workers into the organization at the political, ideological, and psychological levels, they hinder the formation of collectivities that are opposed to it and that challenge once again the logic of capitalism and the practices in which it is rooted.

The power system of the organization also appears as a response to the unconscious contradictions felt by workers in a process of collective work, notably in their impossibility of overcoming an infantile dependence that is transferred onto the organization, limiting their possibilities of cooperation. If the organization influences collective unconscious structures, it is also produced by them in a process of circular reinforcement. Both types of determination define the socio-mental state at a certain stage of its development.

Without wanting to carry out an overly axiomatic symbiosis between the cultural system internal to the transnational and the overall cultural system, let us simply say that what happens in this microcosm has, all the same, many possibilities of projecting itself towards the outside world at a societal level where its interventions obviously come up against other contradictions and other social actors.

The second study from we have just cited would gain from being linked to the study by Bernard Mennis and Karl Sauvant, one of those rare pieces of research that analyze the degree of national involvement and the integration attitudes of the managerial staffs of transnationals. One of the conclusions they reached after having studied the behavior of multinational managers in West Germany was that "managers with international work responsibilities tend to perceive their personal well-being as relatively highly dependant upon developments outside their home country, and they also tend to expect that their well-being is benefited by increased integration. This diminished home-country dependency, furthermore, is associated apparently with somewhat weakened national involvements, although the relationship here is not conclusive. In this context it should be remembered that we have argued elsewhere that even if national involvement is not altered, it is conceivable that regional identifications, as expressed in attitudes regarding integration, are strengthened—that is 'multinational loyalties'."[109]

Other multinational enterprise values have been also singled out in a study carried out by the Canadian government on foreign investment in Canada. These values overflow the strict framework of the internal functioning of the enterprise and constitute elements of a philosophy of development and of the environment it fits into:

> . . . individual responsibility; equalisation of opportunity; social and geographic mobility [i.e., free enterprise system] ideological opposition to state intervention (except for protection from "unfair" competition); use of the employer-employee relationship (e.g. collective bargaining) rather than general legislation to achieve certain social goals; skill training;

growth and expansion of output; exploitation of resources as soon as discovered; technological advance; planned obsolescence; product innovation
and differentiation; increased consumption through mass marketing techniques, including want creation and "hard sell" advertising if necessary;
emphasis on packaging and branding.[110]

We will return to some of these points because in the evaluation of the
impact of transnationals on host societies, the nomenclature of certain sociocultural investments will also appear. The most interesting aspect is
undoubtedly the sociocultural investment represented by the contribution
of technology and cultural capital included in high-level technical know-
how, sophisticated methods, and accumulated experience. This includes not
only the technology to which the transnational has recourse in the process
of the production of material goods and services, but equally the technologies
that it unloads onto the market. In this respect I would simply like to restate
some of the points I made in the introduction on the importation of modern
communication technologies that could well be veritable models of power
organization. These technologies of communication will be increasingly determinant because they propose, in the long run, a total remodeling of
institutions, which constitutes, without any doubt, the most important of
their sociocultural investments. As I wrote in 1977: "It is obviously understood that technology is not only the infrastructure, since the model according to which it is introduced is suprastructural. Moreover, as far as
communications technology is concerned, it conveys messages that are actually standards of behavior."[111] As to the sociocultural investment they
represent, all technologies are not to be put on the same level, for some play
a greater part in the modeling of the social framework in which the others
will eventually fit into.

Content of Cultural Commodities

In 1976 the non-aligned Countries, meeting in New Delhi to discuss the
New International Information Order (NIIO) with a goal to putting an end
to the imbalance in the flow of world information, declared: "The means
of communicating information are concentrated in a handful of
countries. . . . The majority of the world's people are reduced to knowing
each other and themselves through the intermediary of these agencies." The
meeting crowned, in fact, a long struggle of protest with a view to appro-
priating the means of producing its own image and reproducing the values

and ways of life that found and accompany a national and regional process of self-determination. Since the end of the 1960s, on the wave of this new phase of decolonization, numerous studies have appeared on the content of cultural commodities massively dumped on the periphery. Many of these studies have appeared in Latin America, analysing daily life, the situation of women and children, and the social relations between different people and groups proposed by comics, television series, and women's magazines. In 1972, in a demystification of the stereotyped universe of Walt Disney productions, Ariel Dorfman and I considered the image a young Western or even Latin-American reader could have of his or her Latin American brothers and sisters by analyzing a number of episodes in Aztecland, Inca-Blinka, and San Banador:

> All these examples are based upon common international stereotypes. Who can deny that the Peruvian (Inca Blinca TB 104) is somnolent, sells pottery, sits on his haunches, eats hot peppers, has a thousand year old culture— all the dislocated prejudices proclaimed by the tourist posters themselves? Disney does not invent these caricatures, he only exploits them to the utmost. By forcing all peoples of the world into a vision of the dominant (national and international) classes, he gives this vision coherency and justifies the social system on which it is based. These clichés are also used by the mass culture media to dilute the realities common to these people. The only means that the Mexican has of knowing Peru is through cari-cature, which also implies that Peru is incapable of being anything else, and is unable to rise above this prototypical situation, imprisoned as it is made to seem, within its own exoticism. For Mexican and Peruvian alike, these stereotypes of Latin American peoples become a channel of distorted self-knowledge, a form of self-consumption, and finally, self-mockery. By selecting the most superficial and singular traits of each people in order to differentiate them, and using folklore as a means to "divide and conquer" nations occupying the same dependent position, the comic, like all mass media, exploits the principal of sensationalism. That is it conceals reality by means of novelty, which not incidentally, also serves to promote sales. Our Latin American countries become trash cans being constantly repainted for the voyeuristic and orgiastic pleasures of the metropolitan nations. Every day, this very minute, television, radio, magazines, newspapers, films, clothing, and records, from the dignified gab of history text books to the trivia of daily conversation, all contribute to weakening the international solidarity of the oppressed. We Latin Amer-icans are separated from each other by the vision we have acquired of each other via the comics and other mass culture media. This vision is nothing

less than our own reduced and distorted image. This great tacit pool overflowing with the riches of stereotype is based upon common clichés, so that no-one needs to go directly to sources of information gathered from reality itself. Each of us carries within a Boy Scout Handbook packed with the commonplace wisdom of everyman.[112]

An insipid dehistorization is the rule in products of mass culture. As an analyst of tourist advertising in West Africa noted: "It is comic to remark that while tourist advertisements feel obliged to portray the historical contacts between Europe and Africa in all their violence (slavery, colonization), they also simultaneously erase them. These offhand, soothing caricatures of a past of struggle and oppression show a certain contempt for tourists, to whom reassurances must be given, even if they seem contradictory: their compatriots always behave themselves in Africa. Admittedly they did behave badly in the past, but the Africans have already forgotten."[113]

The tourist industry, which materializes numerous stereotypes and prejudices that circulate in film, television, and editorial discourses, is particularly predisposed to carry out reconstitutions of history. In 1980, Christian shareholders in Gulf and Western, owner of a vast tourist complex in the Dominican Republic, denounced this type of practice. "Waiters' work would not be degrading if they did not have to imitate a style of domestic service that brought back memories of serfs or slaves." This is the impression one gets from the luxurious "Casa de Campo" (where the majority of rooms cost $100 a day) when one sees the employees (porters, assistants, gardeners, cleaners, cooks, bellboys, etc.). The most obvious proof of this is in the clothing that reminds one of the former workers and inhabitants of colonial plantations.[114] Evaluating the staff training program, the Christian report added: "Despite the company's good intentions to create 'the greatest possibilities towards progress,' it may well be creating an atmosphere in which employees try to obtain tips and satisfy the whims of wealthy foreigners, instead of being oriented toward their own country's development needs."

Trying to summarize the set of dominant values in the production of mass culture in Latin America, Luis Ramiro Beltran and Elisabeth Fox based on studies undertaken between 1970–79 drew up the following list: individualism, elitism, racism (to which one could add ethnocentrism), adventurism, conservatism, conformism, the feeling of inferiority among the dominated classes, fatalism, authoritarianism, romanticism, and aggressiveness. They summarized "individualism" thus: "The belief that the needs and aspirations of the individual predominate over those of the community to which he or she belongs." Conservatism was defined as "the belief that the socio-economic structures characteristic of capitalism constitute the only desirable and natural social order and that as such, they must be indefinitely maintained for the good of all."[115]

All these values are like satellites of a central planet: the integration into the world of consumption. For the transnational model, the only possibility of "cultural democratization" is through the market. Here, we touch on the nerve point of the conception presiding over so-called mass culture. This culture has become "the vulgarised superstructure of the capitalist mode of production. Above all, this culture represents a lifestyle, forming a unique and coherent totality which creates daily standards that contribute to supporting the dynamics of consumption and production."[116]

Transnational advertisers define advertising as "merely a tool and a technique. It can equally well be used to promote materialism or asceticism, the purchase of cosmetics or US bonds, the sale of smut or scriptures."[117] To reduce advertising to a single technique, tool, or industrial sector amounts to neglecting the very law of the commercial functioning of the media. The advertising spot is one offshoot among others of a system in which advertising is absolute law; in a society based on commodity relations, advertising is the touchstone of the commodity conception of society. In fact, the directors of transnational advertising agencies are far more lucid and in touch with reality when they suggest through a term like "adplomacy," for example, that they are the true and efficient representatives of an economic, political, and social system. Even more sincere are those who define the "democratic market place" as "democracy *tout court.*" This is the case of the president of J. Walter Thompson, who declared in 1972: "During the 27-year period of 1946–1972, advertising volume in the US increased from 3.4 billion to 23 billion, or seven times. This coincides with the greatest economic growth period in American history, and not so coincidentally with the period of the greatest advances in social justice in our society. The corollary is in the fact that the growth of other free-world societies seem to run roughly parallel to the growth of their advertising expenditures."[118] Later, the chairman of Batten, Burton Dunstine, and Osborne put it more aggressively: "Democracies with high living standards are at the top of the list of countries spending a high percent of national income on advertising, whereas communist dictatorships with relatively low living standards are at the bottom of the list. Freedom must have its advertising, or else it will surely run into danger." The same company president-cum-transatlantic marketing theorist concludes his declaration of principles elsewhere with this remark: "The

American Marketing System has as its basis that sudden upsurge of the idea of human freedom."[119]

These declarations are refuted by the real situation in many of the peripheral countries today, like Chile where an incredible increase in advertising expenses is accompanied neither with an increase in living standards nor a strengthening of democracy. The gross revenue of J. Walter Thompson, which had left Chile when Allende took power and had returned after the coup, went from $3.8 million to nearly $8 million between 1977 and 1978 (66.4 percent coming from television). As the *New York Times* commented in 1977: "Chile has become a bazaar filled with foreign goods that are snapped up by the well-to-do while millions of workers and their families are living hand-to-mouth."[120] Michael Moffit and Isabel Letellier also reported that "when tariffs were recently lowered on machine tools, one executive told the *Wall Street Journal* that 'we had to give up making an electric welding machine and began selling an imported one. . . . My question is, what are we going to do with these workers? They want the consumer to get the best price, but who is going to be the consumer?' "[121] In Argentina at the height of the repression in 1977, the twenty-fourth largest agency in the world, Marsteller, accepted the task of trying to redress the image of the military regime through a large-scale advertising and public relations campaign. These incoherencies certainly warrant a long discussion, but the principal question lies elsewhere. Let us simply note the fact that behind the advertising and marketing system and the communication system they orient, lies a certain conception of the political functioning of society. It is in the light of this that we must evaluate the sociocultural investments realized by the transnational system of the production and distribution of cultural commodities.

What does this system propose? *A notion of development.* In a study on Brazil, an *Advertising Age* reporter wrote that "sales of cigarettes, automobiles, detergents and cosmetics could be considered good barometers of a country's development."[122] *A notion of communication,* which essentially reduces the communications apparatus to being no more than an apparatus of mass distribution and diffusion. The only form of participation envisaged for the citizen, seen as a citizen-consumer, in this type of democracy is free access to the market. The notion of technological communication, which establishes a normative hierarchy of the other modes that social groups use to communicate between themselves, tends to devalue the networks of communication and solidarity that these groups spontaneously erect. The notion of obsolescence contributes to this idea of a hierarchy of ways of communicating. A new media displaces and devalues another: color television relegates black and white, modes of communication via interposed technologies relegate others. *A notion of organization:* transnational values tend to substitute themselves for mass networks of social organization based on the idea of solidarity and reconstitute other networks based on the necessity of atomizing consumers. The system of mass marketing and distribution proposes an alternative way of organizing the community and articulating the relations between groups and individuals. Undoubtedly the most striking example is that given by political scientists analyzing the application of marketing methods to political campaigns and concluding, "These firms are anti-party, because they tend to become substitutes for the regular party apparatus."[123] Allergic to the alternative of mobilizing those concerned, communications specialists bank everything on techniques of persuasion. When it was necessary to find a solution for "democratizing" education in Brazil, for example, partisans for the purchase of a satellite emphasized: "Tele-education by satellite, even with all its defects, seems to be one of the only possible means of solving the problems of education in this country. One of the options— among others—which we are not free to choose, would be political mobilization of the population, thus transforming education into a veritable national crusade."[124] *A notion of daily life,* wherein the management of free time and the administration of leisure become open to the market and therefore politically neutral. The only function of entertainment is entertainment. Already in the 1940s, Brecht wrote: "Distractions should not contain any element that is part of work. Distractions in the interest of production should be dedicated to nonproduction. The individual who buys a ticket to the movies is transformed before the screen into an idler and an exploiter; and since the individual has made himself the object of exploitation, it may be said that he or she is a victim of "*im*-ploitation."[125] *A notion of change:* defined by access to modernity-universality; an idea of change defined more in terms of technological progress and the revolution of the productive forces than in terms of a revolution in attitudes, roles, and behavior. As Michèle Mattelart wrote in regard to the relation between modernity as the ideology of technology and technocracy and the minor, relative changes that can be seen in the image of women projected by transnational products, "It is just as if in order to contain and repress the revolutionary meaning of science and technology and in order to prevent these productive forces from adopting another operational mode, the existing order had to cultivate continuity as well as the permanence of the values and symbols that proscribe behavior and distribute social roles."[126] This notion of modernity goes hand in hand with the idea that the democratic society of tomorrow will give everyone the possibility of access to middle-class values and living standards, guarantor of an *Internationale* of social standing.

3

Sociocultural Impacts of Transnational Firms

This is undoubtedly the most immense problem and on many points the least analyzed. The complexity of this theme makes it fairly difficult to delimit. Several aspects already brought up in the introduction intersect within it; these include the activities of transnational firms and the articulation of these activities with those of the local dominant groups, and eventually the resistance of both dominant and dominated groups. In connection with the effects of culture industries, for example, it is not too much of an exaggeration to say that we are faced with a domain of analysis barely explored. Four researchers from the Institute for Communication Research of Stanford University, in a report written for UNESCO on transcultural audiovisual information, justifiably put forward the following conclusion: "Up till now, research has essentially been concerned with a description of the efforts [possibilities of systems, impact of programs, types of audience reached, and other subjects of the same type], rather than the effects of broadcasting. When research has been carried out on the latter, only short-term or limited [non-generalized] effects have been examined. Given the importance of the problem, and the lack of data, it is hardly surprising that desires or fears have been taken for reality on many occasions. The ecstasies and the horrors of the 'global village' have been abundantly depicted, but never seriously supported."[1] The very term *effects* can be interpreted in different ways, and the fact that research on effects requires more and more an interdisciplinary approach is not irrelevant to the relative lack of studies in this domain.

In the following section, I will try to approach this question from four principal questions: What do the few studies on the reception of the medias tell us? What effect do the activities of transnational firms have on consumption patterns? What effects do these firms have on the components of working-class culture? What effect on the situation of women? The second question will be the central one.

Influence of Television

In 1978 at the third Advertisers' Congress at São Paulo, representatives of the large advertising agencies made "a bold appeal to the military government by urging free elections and a return of civil guarantees suspended since 1968."[2] The delegates also demanded that "the government end its prior censorship policy, now compulsory for all ads on radio, TV and cinema." Here is an example of how the activities of transnational firms can lead to democratic demands. Another example: in South Africa in 1977, J. Walter Thompson set up a Black Communications Unit, with a black in charge. Although the official policy of the government was one of apartheid, the company decided to promote a policy of interracial harmony in order to win over the black population, which represents 25 percent of the purchasing power in the cities. This policy was justified as follows: "There are no written laws against integrated ads, so the government probably would not take umbrage at such symbolic breaches of apartheid policies. The nation's business interests, the people controlling the economy, have in fact relatively little to say as to how South Africa is governed. The reasons why lie deep in the country's history. . . . Yet it seems that the English-speaking business community will make a substantial contribution to social change if only because commercial TV comes to South Africa next year. Around the world, TV advertising has proven to be a powerful acculturation tool. It probably will be no less so in South Africa, especially if integrated advertising is soon to come."[3]

Such examples, to which we could add others (correspondents of AP or UPI expelled for doing their jobs in a military dictatorship, etc.) show us to what extent we must be careful when we judge the impact of transnational products on a society. A fundamental distinction must be made: societies with strong, authoritarian regimes, and those developed on the keynote of civil society according to the more or less applied norms of liberal democracy. Transnational cultural products are born in societies governed by the liberal doctrine of information, based on the belief that a consensus must be constructed in order to integrate the various social strata. When these transnational products or cultural agents are in a situation marked by authoritarianism, some of them are likely to enter into contradiction with the context of nonliberal censorship in which they are received. The protests arising from these transnational agents illustrate as much a disagreement with measures vexing the free flow of information as a discontent caused by the impossibility of reaching consumers. However, this explicit protest against authoritarian norms tends to last only as long as the barrier separating the transnational agent from consumers continues to exist. Modern military regimes constructed on economic models strongly influenced by the idea that the economy must be run by large private groups rather than the state, cannot really repeat the experience of the pre-1945 authoritarian regimes, particularly the Nazi regime.[4] After a phase of open warfare against the "internal enemy" and a phase of intense propaganda or psychological warfare, these regimes, particularly that of Chile, delegate the ideological function reserved for the Ministry of Propaganda in the Nazi regime to the private sector and to the medias, guided by a commercial rationality. In Argentina, for example, the military junta decided in 1980 to "privatize" the radio and television channels that had been nationalized under the previous Peronist government. On the economic level, this measure conforms to the desire expressed by the government in 1979 to accelerate the process of privatization of a good part of the 308 enterprises in which the government has interests. At a certain stage in the existence of a military regime, once opposition has been reduced, the apparent contradiction we pointed out above tends to disappear. The ideology of consumerism becomes for those sectors of the population that do not benefit from the economic model, that is, the extensive working-class majority, a mechanism for political mind control. That which one only detects beneath the surface in the present evolution of liberal-democratic states, here breaks out in full daylight. The delegation of the ideological function (or at least a part of it, as psychological warfare continues to constitute the supreme and overdeterminant norm of the military state) to the commercial sector goes hand in hand with the strengthening of the repressive power of the state. The army and police are endowed with the most sophisticated communication and information technologies in the context of a permanent "state of exception."

One must therefore be extremely sceptical of the pretensions of transnational firms "of being a force for change against the excesses" of authoritarian regimes. The behavior of transnational firms in South Africa speaks for itself. Elisabeth Schmidt has sifted through these pretensions.[5] She has systematically analyzed how the "Sullivan code,"—whose principles recommended equal wages for identical tasks, the professional training and promotion of African executives, as well as the construction of decent housing for black workers—has been applied by the American firms installed in South Africa. When the code was promulgated, only half the firms concerned had accepted the principle. According to the last monitoring questionnaire (at the end of 1979), no more than a third had made satisfactory progress towards putting it into practice. Another document, published in London, gave similar results for British enterprises, recalling that according to the British minster of commerce, thirty-three enterprises paid starvation wages and contravened the good conduct code developed in Brussels by the E.E.C. countries with the same intentions as the "Sullivan Code" in the United States.[6]

Once this distinction between the impact in civil societies and the impact in authoritarian societies has been made, we can now examine the results of several studies carried out on television reception. The first study comes from Professor Santoro of Venezuela, who has investigated the formation of stereotypes and the decodification of clichés by young television watchers. Some of his conclusions: for children in their last year of primary school, the "good guys" are the North Americans. The "baddies" come from other countries, particularly Germany and China. The goodies are white, rich, and unmarried and generally work as detectives, police men, or soldiers. The "thugs" are black and poor and work as servants or workers. Good or bad, most heros have English-sounding names. In the cases where the children use a Spanish name, it is to designate the "baddies." The majority of the stories imagined by the children take place almost exclusively in the United States. These stereotyped characters are endowed with a number of qualities: money, prestige, beauty, health, recreation, and success, all of which predominate over intellectual success, cultural development, spiritual elevation, and social solidarity. The author concludes: "Are these the types of attitudes that we wish our children to develop? Must these ideas and messages determine the development of our children? Is this the society to which we aspire? Does this best suit the development of our nation?"[7]

The second study was carried out in Santiago, Chile, by Michèle Mattelart and Mabel Piccini.[8] It emphasizes an elementary fact that tends to be forgotten: time spent watching television is time taken away from other possible activities and social mobilization, particularly in periods which favor working-class mobilization. The authors mention, for example, the problems and intrusions that sometimes came up in womens' organizations when their activities and meetings coincided with certain television programs. Along the same lines, a director of a Chilean rank and file organization remarked: "Currently, television is a factor of permanent demobilization. Because they spend their time watching television and being drenched in bourgeois ideology, these comrades don't participate in organizations and become used to no longer struggling. Although we are making efforts to arouse the interest of the worker in the construction of badly needed houses, television shows him a car, and unfortunately he begins to think about it too much. Television undoes work done elsewhere."

Recognizing that television brings elements of knowledge with it, a large part of the television audience, among the most enlightened sectors of the working class, deplore the fact that this knowledge is often very removed from their own experience. The authors quote the observation of a woman who clearly expresses this reaction and also the impossibility of defining the contribution of a piece of information without referring it to the concrete necessities of the television audience: "We are surprised and openmouthed when we see films about great discoveries, but we don't even know how our men work or the work methods in the coal mines, for example. We know more about astronauts than miners."

The possible critical attitude of consumers to television programing indicates the difficulty of accepting a unilateral notion of effects that fixes the consumer in a passive role. *Active consumption* can occur, when the individual reader or television watcher reacts critically to the messages proposed and creates antidotes. However, one should not use this nuance to relativize the impact of the means of mass communication. They remain powerful means of social control, and we can conclude with many others that their action is exercised to prevent this critical consciousness.

Consumption Patterns

Computers and Importation of a Technology-Consumption Pattern

On several occasions, I have insisted on the importance of new communications systems. I have also suggested in analyzing the transnational TV network how a technology consumption pattern has slid into the initial institutionalization models of the radio-television apparatus. I have also pointed out how, in turn, a marketing system creates in certain developing countries its own configuration of a televisual apparatus, following the density of the advertising flow. I will limit myself here to clarifying a little this other network of dependence that signs away the future of modern information and communications systems. There are few analyses on this theme that attempt to take stock on the situation of developing countries in respect to data processing industry. The rare studies existing have arisen recently in countries wishing to establish a policy of national independence (cf. a Brazilian engineer's declaration to the IBI (Intergovernmental Bureau for Informistics) Congress in Rome). It is in this spirit that computer scientists of the Mexican Ministry of Programming and the Budget presented a report to the first Latin American conference on information science held at Caracas early in 1980.[9] The report related the history of liabilities of computerization, of which all future policies must take heed. The authors show how the commercial policy of six transnational enterprises controlling the Mexican market (IBM with over 55 percent, followed by Honeywell, Univac, Burroughs, NCR, and CDC, ranging from 15 percent to 4 percent of the market respectively), "imposed a product without a local demand by selling solutions to 'problems' they had themselves defined." If we look at the rhythm of growth of the number of computers in Mexico, we can see that on a comparative scale of 1 to 100, the pattern of computer consumption is similar to that of the United States despite the fact, as these computer scientists point out, that national necessities should have imposed a totally different model of use. This consumption pattern, created in a captive market, has instigated a whole chain of dependence, for the physical and logistic maintenance of computing systems is equally controlled by the suppliers. From this stem deficiencies in academic training in this domain; there is a lack of people formally prepared and yet, on the other hand, a proliferation of technicians trained by the suppliers themselves. The latter dispense a training that is limited to the knowledge of their own product. In this way the supplier with the best training centers has the highest share of the market.

The penetration and acceptance of microcomputers was limited until 1976 precisely because their mode of application and social usage were different from those implanted by the large computer suppliers. Thus, in 1977 the national computer infrastructure, which had undergone uncontrolled growth, was made up of more than 2,250 computers of various models, most of which were incompatible with one another. In the public administration sector, for example, there were no less than 142 different models installed in the 230 public administration branches. The consequence of this was "to prevent the development of the market for the nascent computer industry [of Mexico], and to present a grave risk, as representatives of foreign firms operating in the country controlled the functioning of the equipment with which basic and strategic information for the country's administration were treated. Furthermore, the exchange of resources and information between the various institutions became complicated." This example illustrates how a technology development model "has been imposed from beginning to end by the commercial interests of technology sellers who have lead the country into an unbalanced consumption without taking into account the objectives of the use of their technology. Progress was measured by the newness of models, the number of machines installed, and their size and capacity."

Infant Foods Industry

The introduction of one object creates the necessity for a chain of objects that are part of the same structure. It leads to the mode of social and economic organization in which this object is born. In this elementary principle lies the nonneutrality of objects, the supposed neutrality of objects being the foundation of technocratic development ideologies. This is, undoubtedly, the main contribution of the analyses arising since the beginning of the 1970s, which have questioned the policies of transnational firms in respect to imported milk powder and bottle feeding. The best known of these studies, *The Baby Killer,* appeared in 1974. Following this study, Nestlé took judicial action, one in connection with the title (the German translation was even more explicit, *Nestlé Kills Babies*), another contesting that Nestlé's marketing strategies contravened ethical rules, and a third refusing the accusation that in the promotion of Nestlé products, it had improperly used paramedical bodies. These depositions were withdrawn by Nestlé except that concerning the booklet's title. (Developing countries count for 33 percent of Nestlés sales.)

   Numerous studies have followed, illustrating the damage done by the use of infant formula milk to the health of children. Let us cite one of the latest, carried out in September 1979 in the Arab Republic of Yemen, which showed that milk powder lost all nutritional value in being overly diluted to comply with the local belief that an overly "heavy" diet was harmful to babies. Moreover, the child lost a great deal of physical contact with its mother, being abandoned to bottle-feed itself as soon as it was old enough. Finally, the hygiene conditions in which the babies' bottles were prepared and kept were defective and harmful to the babies' health.[10] The same affirmations and denunciations have been made in numerous African countries and in Latin America, particularly in the Dominican Republic.

The Swiss anthropologist, Dominique Perrot, reflecting on new modes of domination through objects on the basis of these cases (Nestlé and others), shows how when the object is introduced alone, it can produce in a determined environment, devastating effects. She also shows how this object constitutes a link in the proposition of a so-called modern life-style and of a style of consumption that these populations cannot attain but which, meanwhile, destroys traditional uses.

> Roughly speaking, what mothers need to correctly use baby bottles is a Western-style kitchen with stove, refrigerator, drinking water, detergents, various containers, and time. At least, this is what is suggested in advertising and explanations concerning the preparation of baby bottles. Thus, a network of signification is constituted and exported with the baby bottle. Women, in buying it, obtain as a free gift what they need in order to base their material aspirations on the mode of the bourgeoisie of industrialized societies. Knowing that this style of life and consumption is out of their economic reach, in their immediate future in any case, they fall back on the baby bottle, which seems to be within their means. It becomes the sign of an accession, on the level of the imaginary, to the modern Western world, which alone pretends to offer the best to its children. . . . As an object-sign, the baby bottle becomes a canal, relating society to the products, language, and values of a multinational. The significations conveyed by the baby bottle are: Nestlé is for the babies' good/using the baby bottle is to be modern, scientific, hygienic, Western, therefore prestigious/the baby bottle is used by the rich, therefore it is desirable/developed women use them/the baby bottle makes them strong, healthy, big, happy, intelligent/a mother who loves her baby buys Lactogene. . . . Finally, the baby bottle also works as a screen: between mother and child, mother and her own body (the sexual taboo imposed on breast-feeding women, who delay ovulation for a period of up to eighteen months, is no longer respected.)[11]

For many firms, concern for the appropriateness of nutritional needs appears secondary. At least, this is what must be concluded when one reads the following suggestions extracted from *Business International* (August 6, 1978):

> Strike their eyes and flatter their sense of color; make the product recognized and without using words, make them want to adopt the brand. In regions

where illiteracy is widespread, a drawing or symbol characteristic of the
brand can be a big help; create your own means of advertising when the
country doesn't have any—for example, films or sound trucks; orient advertising towards women, who are the main consumers; chose the media
most suitable for penetrating the countryside—in largely illiterate rural
areas, the radio is sometimes the most efficient means of communication;
try to give your products a Westernised appearance to give them social
standing in regions undergoing rapid development wherein ideas of modernization and Westernization are linked.[12]

It is in connection with the introduction of milk powder and babies'
bottles that strategies of communication linked to the creation of a demand
have been best analyzed. To give an idea of the bombardment to which
Nestlé subjected certain African countries in 1973–74 to create a demand
for Lactogene, let us cite the case of Sierra Leone (135 thirty-second advertisements were broadcast by the Sierra Leone Broadcasting Service in August
1974 alone) or of Kenya (where for three weeks in 1973 11 percent of radio
advertising in Swahili was devoted to Lactogene).[13] These advertising
sledgehammer strategies set up the medical and paramedical organizations
as the guarantees of the products of nutrition firms. In a report submitted
to UNICEF and WHO, Pierre Borgoltz correctly remarks that the characteristics of the promotion of milk powder were considerably different from
those of ordinary food consumption goods. The introduction and adoption
of milk powder and babies' bottles were legitimized by the special status
of "quasi-prescription drugs" that these products took on.[14] It is worthwhile
recalling that the transnational industry controlling the infant formula is
extremely concentrated.[15] Eighteen companies supplied more than 95 percent
of this product on the market, and the five largest accounted for 75 percent
of this total. The largest of them, Nestlé, alone supplies more than 30
percent of world production.

Certain transnational firms, trying to find the right answer to the various
protests against the indiscriminate use of publicity for milk powder, have
responded by promulgating their own code of ethics. In November 1975,
Nestlé, a Danish firm, four Japanese firms, a British firm, and an American
firm formed ICIFI (International Council of Infant Food Industries). Four
other companies joined this group soon afterwards; the French firm, BSN-
Gervais-Danone and three Dutch firms. The secretary of this body is the
former deputy director-general of WHO. In this code we read, "Product
information for the public will always recognize that breast milk is the
feeding of choice with the recommendation to seek professional advice when

a supplement or alternative may be required."[16] Afterwards, several companies (including Nestlé), following the example of Bristol Myers and de Wyeth, also produced their own code. The way in which these codes are respected is extremely contested by IBFAN (International Baby Food Action Network), which is the umbrella group for numerous protest organisations, above all in Europe and the United States. In December 1980, representatives of IBFAN stressed to WHO that "ICIFI companies violated their own ethical guidelines at least 400 times in the past 18 months. They also violated a pledge made at a WHO conference last year not to place advertisements in Third World mass media, including newspapers, magazines and billboards."[17]

The reactions of transnational firms to the campaigns of organizations denouncing their practices in the Third World have been extremely virulent and equal to the damage these campaigns cause to their vital interests. In "The Corporation Haters," in the June 6, 1980 issue of *Fortune,* appeared the following:

The spirit of the New Left lives on in an anti-business coalition, sponsored by none other than the National Council of Churches. . . . For the radicals, the alliance with church groups has many other tangible advantages. It provides a way of conducting political programs behind the shield of tax exemption, and access to a large organizational network. The church activists can gather information from missionaries throughout the world and disseminate propaganda to the memberships of participating churches. Above all, the religious connection provides respectability and legitimacy. What better way to challenge the existing system than to brand it as an offense to the will of God?

In order to attract broad support, the church activists have chosen to present business-related issues as morally clearcut and simple—when in fact they are usually complex, morally ambiguous, and involve difficult policy trade-offs. How moral, for example, is the pursuit of a boycott strategy that might help bring about an apocalyptic racial war of liberation in South Africa? A good many black South Africans, who would not be privileged to follow this exciting but bloody drama from comfortable observation posts in the U.S., say that it is neither moral nor wise. Even though the people working on Castle & Cooke's banana plantations in Central America earn far less than the U.S. minimum wage, would they be better off if the company decided to move elsewhere? Is opposition to nuclear power in the U.S. really the only possible moral position when the alternative is more death and disease from the mining and burning of fossil fuels and greater energy problems for the Third World?

But propagandists know that complexity and ambiguity actually feed the demand for simple answers, whether the issue is strip-mining, South Africa, or nuclear power. The infant-formula issue provides perhaps the best example of all as to how this process works.

However, multinationals' own strategies have also profited from such attacks and accusations. Thus, a representative of Ross Laboratories argued that in his opinion "the activists may be doing corporations a good turn by prodding them to prove they can meet social challenges. Thus the Marxists marching under the banner of Christ may help the private enterprise system to adapt and survive—even though that may be the last thing they want to happen."

Protein Myth

However, food products are introduced that are less in the news and attract less virulent criticism. A study published in 1979 was carried out by four economists of the Institute of Studies of Economic and Social Development of the University of Paris.[18] Its object was the analysis of the introduction of Nescafe and Maggi beef cubes by CAPRAL, a subsidiary of Nestlé, in the Ivory Coast. Three conditions make this a paradigmatic case; (1) CAPRAL was established at the request of the Ivory Coast authorities in 1959. The Ivory Coast was characterized by an export-oriented primary economy, with a very limited internal market. The people did not have consumption habits similar to those of developed countries; it was thus a very different situation to that of the first settlements of Nestlé in Latin America, Brazil, and Argentina. When Nestlé established itself in these countries, it found an economy in transition from a primary exporting one to one based on mixed import industry; there was already a relatively large internal market, a development of urban agglomerations where consumption patterns had been imported from the advanced European countries, and a threshold of minimal profitability thanks to a guaranteed solvency. In the Ivory Coast, nothing like this existed. (2) Normal rules, whereby large multinational firms are regulated by the mechanism of competition (the development of innovations, product obsolescence, constant renewal of demand for differentiated products), do not apply in the Ivory Coast. Maintaining a low price for the product was essential. As the authors point out, in an economic space where a radical difference exists between the mode of consumption of the majority and that of the elite, "difference in price and not by differentiation of the product plays an essential role when it is a question of imposing totally new consumption habits and determining which firm will do it." From 1959 to the time of the study, CAPRAL was in this phase and it is only recently that a mechanism of competition by product innovation (for example, the introduction of decaffeinated coffee) has begun to develop. (3) The communications system used is not an overdose system. Having noticed that the normal channels of mass communications did not seem particularly appropriate for creating a need for the new product (soluble coffee) among the people, a special distribution system was organized: trucks brought coffee to the market and prospectors proposed tastings to the public. It was the same for the Maggi cube except that women controlling small markets were used as sales points. According to the authors, the distribution of soluble coffee had the following impact, which can be presented in a double aspect:

> On the one hand, this implied an orientation of a part of the monetary revenue—usually very limited—towards a product that from a strictly biological point of view, made a feeble nutritional contribution. However, consideration only from the biological point of view remains extremely insufficient, especially if we take into account the fact that coffee is above all a stimulant. It has effects on the behavior of consumers, which must lead to a psycho-social analysis of the effects of coffee consumption. On the other hand, coffee has become the basis of a new form of alimentation that seems to replace the midmorning meal, made up of starch spiced with peppers and sauces, by a form of breakfast with a higher calorie content, notably condensed milk and sugar, and increasingly in urban areas, bread. If this new diet seems more satisfactory from a biological point of view, it should not be forgotten that it is based on imported products, thus leading to a food dependency on the exterior.[19]

In 1975 Nestlé began production of dehydrated stock, known under the name of Maggi cube, with relatively spectacular results. Beginning on January 1, 1976, the manufacture of Maggi cubes in the Ivory Coast gave total sales for that year of 380 million cubes for a population of seven million; (500 million cubes were envisaged for 1977). If we assume an average of ten people per household, this means that each household will consume seven hundred cubes a year or two a day. As the authors note, the Maggi cube has become a staple in the Ivory Coast. However, the distribution of the Maggi cube raises problems similar to those arising with the introduction of soluble coffee. It has the following effects on the food development model: (1) the creation of a dual dependence in regard to the exterior, a technological dependence (nontransferable technology monopolized by a foreign firm) and an import dependence, as imported raw materials must be added to local raw materials. (2) The population puts in its shopping basket a product with a base of vegetable proteins in a nutritional environment that is lacking in animal proteins. The authors emphasize that the Maggi cube was thought up in a European context in the nineteenth century to provide for groups and classes with meager resources. Arguing that a deficiency of amino acids results from the non-consumption of animal proteins, Nestlé has carried out research in its Vevey laboratory to enrich the cube, in the same way that it is making soluble in its Maryland laboratories a type of coffee called Arabusta experimentally grown in the Ivory Coast. However, the blending in of amino acids "is likely to reinforce still more food dependence on the exterior. In effect, the production of synthetic amino acids requires an extremely developed technology. Only several large multinational firms in the world are capable of producing them. Consequently, one of the important conditions of nutritional balance depends on multinational firms."[20]

We are once again faced with finding a solution to a problem transnationals have themselves defined, that is, finding proteins and incorporate them into their own food products in order to resolve the malnutrition problem of a developing country. Increasingly nutritional circles contest this way of seeing things. As James Austin said in 1976, "Protein fortification is an expensive way to solve a calorie problem." Sukhatme adds, "There is no evidence to support the thesis that diets common in developing countries are deficient in protein. Rather, the limiting factor is calories to utilise the protein eaten, and not the protein itself."[21] It is increasingly asserted in these circles that the emphasis placed on the protein question over the last decades was a myth that has led to a fiasco. This is the balance sheet established by three anthropologists in November 1980 (Diener, Moore, and Mutaw), who did not hesitate to speak of a "tragic mistake." In their approach, a critique of the whole food industry controlled by conglomerates unfolds. The food industry still depends today on the same protein myth in order to promote all-beef pet food, or high-protein hair shampoo. These anthropologists also attack the idea that the evolution of a food consumption pattern in the privileged West, which has meat, has been natural. Quoting one of their colleagues, they point out: "In short, the idea that the meat cult has grown up spontaneously in the West, in response to "public demand"—a demand, furthermore, that is supposed to be engraved by evolution on our psyche—is ludicrous. Meat has been sold . . . as assiduously as any other commercial product. . . . History does not show that the West's modern carnivorousness is rooted in anything deeper than commercial expediency. . . . The same line of argument explains our predilection for other manifestations of value adding—tea, coffee, tobacco, sugar, and the rest."²²

The protein myth is still alive and well. Witness the initiative of Coca-Cola, which in May 1978 launched in Mexico a new drink, Samson, "with proteins." Advertising agencies for Coca-Cola used in their advertisements the list of recommendations made by the National Institute of Nutrition for the feeding of school-age Mexican children. They linked Coca-Cola's initiative to a campaign for public health. The disavowal of the Institute was not long in coming; through a spokesman it refuted Coca-Cola's propaganda: "It is false that Coca-Cola is contributing towards a better nutrition for the Mexican people, and even more false that Samson has seven vitamins, niacin, folic acid, calcium, and phosphorous, as its propaganda pretends. . . . The ideal situation would be to lessen the consumption of fizzy drinks in the country and attain a balanced diet of eggs, meat, and milk. This drink's image runs the risk of becoming generalized, giving the false impression that fizzy drinks are nutritious, and diverting the objectives of education and government programs of reorientating Mexican eating habits. The contents of Samson contain one fifth of the protein value of one egg."²³

Agribusiness Complex

In Latin American countries, the influence of transnational firms on food consumption patterns is exercised in a specific way. Since the 1960s agribusiness has been trying to integrate the food system of South American countries into those of the advanced capitalist countries. Thus, a transnational system is organised, affecting the production and distribution of foodstuffs and other products based on agricultural raw materials.

According to data supplied by the UN Study Center on Transnational Firms,²⁴ of the 161 largest food firms operating in 1976, eighty-nine had their headquarters in the United States, twenty-six in Great Britain, six in Canada, fourteen in Japan, two in Australia, two in South Africa, one in Argentina, and the other twenty-one in various West European countries. About 25 percent of the takings realized overseas by transnational firms in this sector came from their subsidiaries in peripheral countries. However, if we take the six largest food firms in the world, that is, those with revenue from food exceeding three billion dollars in 1977 (Unilever, Nestlé, Kraft, General Foods, Esmark, Beatrice Foods), the foreign revenue reaches 41 percent. Firms with their headquarters in the United States have two-thirds of their investments and 90 percent of their production in the Western hemisphere (in particular, Mexico, Brazil, Venezuela, Colombia, Peru, and Central America) and in the Philippines. The great majority of the investments of British firms in the periphery are found in Africa and Asia. Among the other European firms, only Nestlé has a network extending to all continents; some French transnational firms have subsidiaries in former colonial territories in Africa, and Japanese subsidiaries are above all concentrated in Asia, even though in the 1970s they increased their activity in Latin America and Africa. Of the Latin American countries, Mexico and Brazil received nearly 65 percent of the total American food investments in 1977.

The penetration of food transnationals is undoubtedly at its most advanced in Mexico: 130 foreign enterprises own over 300 industrial establishments, of which 80 percent are of North American origin.[25] However, paradoxically, Mexico has to import over half of the basic food elements needed by the population (wheat, beans, sorghum, corn). Participants at the fifth World Congress on Rural Sociology, held in Mexico in August 1980, drew up a picture of the extent of the control of the food industry in Mexico by transnational firms. In the tobacco industry, their dominance is total; in the development of veterinary products, prepared foods, and the ownership of patents for fertilizer manufacture, they control 90 percent of the industry; in the insecticide and pesticide industries, they control 95 percent. Transnationals also control 93 percent of the tractor industry and the agricultural machinery industry; 75 percent of oils and vegetables; 70 percent of the packaged food industry, drinks, and desserts; 65 percent of the chocolate and sweets industry; and 65 percent of the pulp and paper industry. They take part in 35 percent of the selling and commercialization of food products.[26]

Mexico is also one of the peripheral countries where one finds the highest incidence of fast-food restaurants. In 1976 it had as many as all the other countries of Central America put together. In Brazil on the other hand, the penetration of McDonalds, for example, following that of chains belonging to Nestlé, only dates from 1979.[27]

If we leave out public service advertising, it is transnational food firms that contribute the most to advertising investment in Mexico. In 1979 they financed 14.6 percent of television advertising with a total broadcast time of 112,530 seconds for the month of August 1979 alone: thirty-four food and drink firms contributed to this advertising investment; 68 percent of them were transnationals.[28] Numerous studies have been carried out to analyse the evolution of the diet of different Mexican classes. The conclusion of one of them, carried out between 1976 and 1979, was as follows: "The evolution of the food industry examined in each of the forty classes making up the food sector allows us to conclude that a tendency exists towards the production of extravagant food. We speak of extravagant consumption not only because it is a question of foods consumed as a matter of preference by the richest social strata but also because the foods sometimes have an extensive market among the middle or lower strata and are not necessary for a good diet; on the contrary, the expense involved in their purchase means that the lower classes are sacrificing the consumption of basic food products that are essential for the human diet."[29] The authors of this study, the Mexican counterpart of research undertaken on a continental scale by the Chilean economist, Gonzalo Arroyo, have analyzed the growth of each category of firms. They note that the most surprising growth, between 1970 and 1975, was that of the manufacture of crisps and other similar corn-based products, which began to be developed by transnational subsidiaries towards 1965. Four establishments dominated this category, including two subsidiaries of Pepsi and one of Kellogs. These are, the authors affirm, enterprises which, "thanks to expensive advertising campaigns accompanied by an excellent distribution system, probably similar to that for drinks, have given these products of feeble nutritional value an expansion without precedent." The authors also point out, even though it is widely known, that the diet of the poorest classes, essentially made up of corn, beans, fats, and oil, has deteriorated the most. The consumption of drinks and desserts has increased and that of pure sugar has decreased. In other words, these complementary calories are consumed in a more developed and expensive form. In the middle and higher strata, animal proteins—meat, milk, and its derivatives—predominate and the consumption of wheat is greater than that of corn.

The installation of this food production pattern in Mexico tends to be reproduced throughout the whole continent. This was also the conclusion of Salvador Allende's former minister of agriculture, Jacques Chonchol, in 1980: "On the one hand, this pattern marginalizes very small producers who make up the great majority of peasants, as well as landless workers, increasingly made poorer through underemployment, because of the highly intensive technology in the use of capital. On the other, it marginalizes very poor urban and rural consumers, incapable of affording food products with a high added industrial and services value. Even those among the poor who are integrated into this pattern because of a slightly greater purchasing power, have to sacrifice other needs; one could say they pay more to eat less well."[30]

A similar conclusion can be drawn from the national survey of nutrition and alimentation carried out by SAM (Sistema Alimentario Mexicano). A comparison of present-day food consumption with nutritional surveys of the last twenty years allows us to clearly see the substantial changes in consumption patterns, particularly over the last five years. In rural areas, the average consumption of corn per person dropped from 407 grams a day in the 1959–64 period to 324 grams in 1979; beans dropped from 56 to 37 grams over the same period, and bread and pasta increased from 36 to 45 grams. Eggs increased from 15 to 27 grams, milk from 76 to 102 grams, and cooking fat from 14 to 27 grams. In urban areas, the SAM survey came to the conclusion that the consumption of industrialized products, refined flour, and sugar (10 to 30 grams) and drinks (135 to 218 grams) had changed dramatically. The extent of malnutrition in rural areas was such that 90 percent of the population there (21 million people) suffered from calorific and protein underconsumption in one way or another. About 9.5 million of them suffered from a grave calorific deficiency that varied from 25 percent to 40 percent of the minimum norm of 2,700 calories per person per day. In the urban areas surveyed, at least a million people in the federal district consumed less than 2,000 calories a day. The SAM survey also emphasized the damage done by the modernization model from advanced countries that reckons on a pattern of alimentation based on animal protein but with "additives and industrial processing that increase the price of a calorie unit and a gram of protein enormously." It is this pattern of food consumption that has marked out the way for this "breathtaking substitution of sorghum for corn, an accelerated growth in demand for soy beans, and the growing use of corn for animals to the detriment of human consumption, in such a way that Mexico has become a buyer, at increasingly high prices, of what it used to export."[31]

All these studies confirm that the consumption pattern created by the transnational system requires, to draw real benefits from it, a level of income that is only accessible to 20 or 30 percent of the total population.

The American, Robert Ledogar, in the now classic study "Hungry for Profits: U.S. Food and Drug Multinationals in Latin America," has clearly shown the damage done by the artificial drinks produced by Coca-Cola or Pepsi-Cola to the diet of the people. He recalls the observation of a Mexican priest living in one of the most declining areas of the country. "Everything takes place as if fizzy drinks were an important factor in the village's development. I've heard the people of the village say to one another that they cannot stop themselves from drinking them during the day. Some take them with meals to give themselves status, especially if they have guests. . . . Most people have to drink them daily. This is above all because of the enormous amount of advertising, particularly on the radio, which is very much listened to in the mountain regions. At the same time, natural products, like fruit, are consumed less and less—only once a week in some families. Some sell their agricultural products to buy fizzy drinks." This penetration of artificial fizzy drinks is often made at the expense of local drinks made from a natural fruit base. In Brazil, reports Ledogar, Coca-Cola sapped the production of a local fruit-based drink, guarana, by manufacturing the totally artificial Fanta guarana. Whereas the South of Brazil suffers from chronic overproduction of grapes, Fanta grape juice does not contain a single drop of grape juice. Whereas Brazil is the biggest exporter of orange juice in the world, Fanta orange does not contain a single drop of orange juice. However, Coca-Cola is one of the biggest consumers of Brazilian oranges, and large sectors of the Brazilian population suffer from a high vitamin C deficiency.

According to the New Zealand anthropologist, T. F. Ryan[32] even the most isolated Pacific islands have recently become, to varying degrees, integrated into the transnational food network, whereas for the early parts of the modern era, they were in general involved in restricted commercial exchanges only with companies linked to their colonial overlords. The tiny Polynesian society of Niué, for example, came within the New Zealand sphere of influence; thus, surplus cash crops and basketing were exported to New Zealand in return for essential tools, clothes, and a limited amount of food.

Since World War II, however, this picture has changed dramatically. Until the 1950s, Niué was completely self-sufficient in meat and fish production, apart from some imports of canned meat from New Zealand. This canned bully beef is viewed as a status food in most South Pacific cultures. On Niué, for instance, canned corned beef is accorded the same status as traditional locally produced foods in ceremonial feasts or exchanges; a small can is considered to be the equivalent of a chicken, a bird, land crab, or small fish, and a large keg of meat is equal to a pig or large game fish. Now, as the Niueans abandon subsistence production in favor of wage labour on Niué or emigration to New Zealand, the importation of canned meat and other consumer items has increased dramatically. Even more noticeable is the dramatic evolution of imported canned fish.

Ironically, the canned fish that a Polynesian, Melanesian, or Micronesian buys for his dinner may have been caught in the very waters that he himself fished until very recently, and which were fished without competition by his ancestors over the past millenium. Now, in Niué, for example, the number of fishing canoes is only a fraction of what it was a generation ago. After 1952 with the signing of the peace treaty between the United States and Japan, boats from the latter were allowed to venture into the Pacific, followed by Taiwanese and Korean fishing fleets. American capital, responding to the attraction of cheap fish, cheap labour, special tax concessions, and a growing domestic demand for tuna (U.S. households increased their consumption by 320 percent between 1946–61), began to establish canneries in the region. The first was in the trust territory of American Samoa, set up by Van Camp Sea Foods in 1953; ten years later the Star Kist Corporation added another close by. This monoindustry, now worth $100 million annually (up from $33 million in 1970) has had far-reaching effects on Samoan social and economic life: rampant consumerism, the importation of former staples like taro, and the emigration of half the population to Hawaii and the mainland U.S.

However, it would be wrong to think that the governments of these newly independent nations are unaware of these problems. Several at least have taken steps to ensure that the development of industries on their shores should be joint ventures between government and transnational. Most have supported the necessity for the protection of their most abundant resource, the sea, by declaring against U.S. opposition 200 mile fishing zones. At the meeting of the South Pacific Forum in 1978, member nations prevented the U.S. from becoming a member of the proposed Regional Fisheries Organisation.

Pharmaceutical Industry

Ten thousand companies can be described as pharmaceutical manufacturers. However, no more than a hundred have any importance on the international market. These hundred firms supply 90 percent of world supplies of pharmaceutical products. Among them, American firms are largely dominant, as much in number as in volume of sales. Second and third place are occupied by West Germany and Switzerland. The thirty-three firms based in these three countries have about 80 percent of the sales of the top fifty companies. In 1977 the first of the fifty large transnational pharmaceutical firms, Hoechst, obtained 67 percent of its sales volume from overseas; the second, Merck, obtained 44.9 percent; Bayer, 69 percent; Ciba-Geigy, 98 percent; and the fifth, Hoffmann-Laroche, 90 percent. Proportionately it is the industrial sector that is the most involved in the promotion of a transnational commodity. In 1978 approximately 20 percent of all drug sales at the manufacturer's level went for promotion.[33] This proportion is still higher in certain peripheral countries; in Mexico it attains 27 percent of the sales figure of pharmaceutical companies. On the other hand, in this same country these firms invest only 1 percent of their revenue in research, with the consequence that 98 percent of the patents for pharmaceutical products made in Mexico are foreign. Of the forty largest pharmaceutical companies, only three have no foreign capital.[34]

This divergence between the figure allotted for promotion and that allotted to research has given rise to numerous criticisms on the part of peripheral countries, since besides these enormous sums for promotion, there has also been a proliferation of products and brands. The differentiation of products has become alarming in Mexico, "The brand-name system produces a bewildering array of different names for the same drug. . . . The number of products on the market ranges from 8,500 in France to 80,000 in Mexico."[35] This proliferation has direct repercussions on the way in which products are chosen, as much by the doctor as the customer. The best promoted are the most recommended. According to a survey carried out in May 1979 in a small town in the West of the country, 95 percent of prescription drugs were transnational. Doctors justified their choice by invoking "efficiency, their confidence in the product, 'specificity,' and 'economy.' "[36]

The prescription drugs introduced by transnational firms, concentrated on 20 percent of the population, distort the pattern of pharmaceutical consumption; overconsumption of some products among the well-off classes, underconsumption among the others. A survey by the Indian government on the pharmaceutical industry (Hathi Committee, 1975) came to the conclusion "that transnational drug companies are interested in carrying out research only on products which will have a global demand such as tranquilizers, anti-histamines, anti-hypertensives, etc and not on drugs for treatment for tropical diseases. . . . If, in the course of their scheduled research, the drugs synthesized by them show activity against tuberculosis, helminths etc, they are marketed as such."[37]

A Mexican economist, analyzing the development of the health industry in Mexico, came to similar conclusions. Among the ten largest therapeutic firms, which have 55.1 percent of total prescription drug sales in 1976, vitamins are found in second place, representing more than three times as big a market share as drugs against diarrhea and intestinal antiseptics, whereas one of main causes of death in Mexico is precisely this type of disease.[38] The Hathi Committee has also denounced the deployment of marketing methods to the detriment of therapeutic concerns. It pointed out

the damage caused by transnational firms which "block others from producing . . . drugs for a period of 16–20 years by invoking patent protection,
din the brand names into the minds of the medical profession by employing
a large force of medical detailers, resort to high pressure sales techniques
. . . and rig up prices to levels which have no relation to the costs of
manufacture of products or international prices."[39]

What exists in the way of consumer protection? More often than not,
there is one law for the rich and another for the poor. In a survey on
marketing and advertising of medicines and foodstuffs in the Third World,
Charles Medawar has compiled numerous cases where the information supplied to consumers in peripheral countries in the case of medicines was
deficient in relation to that given to central countries. He quotes the observation of Yudkin, who wrote in 1978: "Pediatric preparations of tetracycline are marketed by Lederie, Squibb, Pfizer, Lepetit and Boots without
mention of the possible risks or the recommendation made in Britain, that
tetracycline should not be used in children up to 12 years of age. Liothyronine
('Tertroxin,' Glaxo) is promoted for the treatment of 'lowered metabolic
states' in Africa, contrasting with the British . . . indication of "severe
thyroid deficiency." Methadone ("Physeptons," Burroughs-Welcome) recommended in Britain for severe pain, is included in [the] African [prescribing
guide] as a cough suppressant."[40] Systematically comparing the British
edition of the prescription guide *(Monthly Index of Medical Specialities)* and
the edition circulating in Africa, the West Indies, and the Middle East, the
author came to the conclusion that there are "sometimes serious discrepancies
in the information given by some drug companies in the prescribing guides
used in the U.K. and in the developing countries—and sometimes also in
the guides used in the U.S. and the U.K. In general, the U.K. physicians'
desk reference gave much better and fuller information than did U.K.
MIMS—which in turn generally gave much better and fuller information
than was available in the African, Caribbean and Middle-Eastern MIMS."[41]

Since 1972 several consumers' movements have denounced this propensity
of transnational pharmaceutical firms to lack concern for informing consumers in peripheral countries. In August 1972 the International Organization of Consumers' Unions (IOCU) established the exemplary wrongdoing
of the distribution of chloramphenicol, manufactured by Parke-Davies. For
the first time in the world, a study set out to strongly illustrate in detail
how a transnational firm could commercialize overseas a medicine without
warning (mandatory in the home country) of its dangerous and even fatal

side effects. This study, undertaken in twenty-one countries, affirmed that in no case was information on possible side effects given. What is more, there were wide variations in the warning given with the same brand produced by the same company in different countries. Other products were closely examined, notably clioquinol, which was the object of a report by the same organization in 1975. This product is available in at least fifty countries and without prescription in thirty-nine of them. Whereas it is banned in Japan and the United States, millions of these tablets are still sold under numerous brand names throughout the world. One of the latest surveys carried out in eight Asian countries in 1979 concerned the promotion of sweetened condensed milk, manufactured by Nestlé and Carnation among others. In some countries, it was advertised as a baby food, whereas, in others, its use for babies was contraindicated.[42]

Various feminist movements have also rebelled against the sending of contraceptive products, forbidden by the U.S. Food and Drug Administration for being carcinogenic, to the Third World. One product in particular, manufactured by Upjohn, was often distributed by U.S. foreign aid health organizations: the Depo-Provera. This is injected into large numbers of women in more than seventy countries every year. "It causes 'menstrual chaos' which for some women means dangerously severe bleeding. Complete 'menstrual cessation' follows after several injections. It makes women highly susceptible to infections, diabetes, headaches, depression and dizziness. And in many cases, it causes long-term infertility and perhaps permanent sterility. Since many third world women are breast-feeding or pregnant when they receive the Depo-Provera injection, the dangerous drug is passed on to their children. It causes birth defects such as congenital heart diseases, curvature of the spine, and, in the case of the female foetus, masculinization."[43]

As we have noted in our introduction, not only transnational firms but also foundations, and foreign aid organizations converge in the development of birth-control policies, which, in the past, have often been used experimentally on women in certain Third World countries to test products, which in the United States can only be tested on prisoners; a practice refused by other Western countries concerned with recognising prisoners' rights.[44] As a general rule, the distribution of contraceptives has often been an occasion to depart yet again from the necessity of informing women and for sending high-dosage pills to Third-World countries years after they have been banned by the U.S. Food and Drug Administration, or unsterilized Dakon Shields, whereas local clinics have had no means of sterilizing them.[45]

Runaway Hazardous Shops

What is happening in the domain of the consumption of hazardous and substandard goods, is repeated for the exportation to the Third World of industries representing a danger for workers and the community. We are witnessing the installation of "runaway hazardous shops," to use the expression of Barry Castleman, who for a long time has taken stock of the "export of hazardous factories to developing nations." His diagnosis is clear. "It is inescapable that, as manufacturers in industrial nations are forced to absorb the economic burdens of preventing and compensating occupational and environmental diseases caused by their operations, pressures favouring hazard export will increase. National efforts to implement environmental controls for hazardous industries may have to be complemented by measures that prevent the mere displacement of killer industries to 'export platforms' in nonregulating countries. Poverty and ignorance make communities in many parts of the world quite vulnerable to the exploitation implicit in hazard export."[46] Numerous sectors in the United States or Japan affected by the environmental control measures enacted by their governments have been gone through by Castleman: asbestos textiles and friction products, arsenic and refined copper from primary smelters, mercury mining, pesticides, benzedine dyes, mineral industries in general. Let us give several examples. In 1972, Amatax, a firm based in Norristown, Pennsylvania, closed down their four year old asbestos yarn mill in Millford Square, Pennsylvania, and decided to work solely from its asbestos textile factory established in Agua Prieta, Mexico. It was only in September 1977 that Texas television denounced the damage done. The report showed that workers had not been warned of the danger to their lives by breathing asbestos. Mexico does not have any specific regulation protecting asbestos workers. Another firm, Raybestos-Manhattan took 47 percent of the shares of an asbestos textiles factory in Venezuela in 1974 because "the Venezuelan plant operates at airborne asbestos levels lower than the peak level allowed in the U.S. by the current OSHA (Occupational Safety and Health Administration) standard." In 1976 the Japanese firm, Nippon Asbestos preferred to accelerate its production in Taiwan and South Korea because this industry fell under special legislation in Japan. In January 1975, OSHA proposed to lower the workplace limit for airborne arsenic exposure from 500 to 4 micrograms per cubic meter of air in the light of mounting reports on the carcinogenicity of inorganic arsenic. Arsaco is the sole American producer of arsenic. Once again Mexico served as a dumping ground, then Peru. The case of pesticides, particularly leptophos, manufactured up until 1976 by Velsicol Chemical in Texas, caused a real scandal in November of the same year, when U.S. distribution was banned. This pesticide had been used in Mexico for tomato cultivation destined for U.S. export. The handling of this product proved to be extremely dangerous, according to an expert survey. Leptophos notably led to nervous illnesses. However, the history does not stop there, as afterwards tons of leptophos were sent to Indonesia and other Third World regions under USAID foreign aid programs. The latest case is that of the soil fumigant, dibromochloro-propane (DBCP), produced by Shell Chemical and Dow Chemical, which was banned in 1977 for causing sterility in workers. At the end of 1978, when this product continued to be manufactured in two factories installed in Mexico, the discovery of cases of sterility among Mexican workers led to the closure of the factories. Cut to the quick, *machismo* at least knew how to defend itself! Puerto Rico, which had already been an experimental terrain for the development of birth control policies in Third World countries, is undoubtedly, along with Mexico, one of the countries where the most polluting industries have landed. Let us simply quote several sentences of a Puerto Rican scientist's report, which having shown the effects of the petrochemical industries implanted in the island, denounces the damage done by thermo-electric complexes: "Every minute they discharge onto the coasts 1.2 million gallons of hot water, which, because of its high temperature, destroys plankton, the nutritional base of all marine life. This quantity of hot water equals 50 percent of the waters of all the rivers of Puerto Rico pouring into the sea every minute. . . . In regions subjected to the fumes of the petrochemical complexes, the productivity of sugarcane has decreased considerably in a ratio of 40:13 (according to local measurements) and the proportion of sugar in honey has gone from 9 percent to 2.8 percent."[47]

It must be admitted in all honesty that some companies, by refusing to trade with countries that have not established legislation for the protection of workers and the community against polluting industries, put pressure on host countries for the adoption of adequate measures, with decisive social impact. This is the case of the Johns-Manville Corporation, one of the biggest producers of asbestos fibers in the Western Hemisphere, which includes the following reservation in its sales policy: "We will reserve the right to refuse to sell asbestos fiber to customers who fail to meet applicable governmental regulations on asbestos exposure and thereby endanger the health of their employees, and expose Johns-Manville to unwarranted liability. In countries where there are no governmental regulations on asbestos exposure, accepted industrial hygiene practice shall apply."[48]

Tourist Industry

Numerous authors have emphasized the pernicious aspect of the "shop-window" effect of the tourist industry: the visited tend to adopt the consumption patterns conveyed by the visitors. The importance of the tourist industry in the production of this shop-window effect cannot be exaggerated. If the tourist industry produces this effect, it is as a component of the system of culture industries, and it is difficult to isolate its specific effect from this point of view. The most that can be said is that the tourist industry is liable to constitute the fundamental factor in the creation of this shop-window effect when the other components of the culture industries and the marketing system are less developed than the tourist industry itself. In this case, the tourist industry is promoted to the rank of locomotive for the signs of modernity and mass culture. This was remarked upon in a UNESCO report: "The shop-window effect turns up the mechanisms to which 'sledgehammer advertising' appeals, implying the psychological debilitation of the masses so that an effectively unidirectional conditioning can operate. Tourists do not have these means; only the mass media have them. Generally from now on we wonder if the real agents of the shop-window effect are not the means of information of receptor countries, which thus organize the continuous promotion of the Western consumer society model. . . . Tourism plays a role in this system to the extent that it authenticates media myths, but this role is a fairly secondary one."[49]

If this last point allows us to relativize the specific effects of the tourist industry on consumption patterns for the whole of society, it must, all the same, be added that in high-density tourist zones, the impact of this industry on the consumption patterns of the zone/enclave is very visible. Land speculation and inflation are the most repeated terms used to isolate the effects of the tourist industry. Price rises are also frequent: "In the outskirts of Waza (Cameroun), the price of chicken doubles between the rainy season and the tourist season; bows and spears increased 50 percent during the same period."[50] The local population's basic utensils become tourist souvenirs, which increase in price both for tourists and locals. This is also true of transport, whose relative scarcity increases in the high season. Many authors stress the conflict existing in several tourist zones like the Seychelles between tourism and agriculture, where the displacement of the latter aggravates dependence on imported food, both for tourists and the local people.[51] Without, however, erecting tourism into the principal cause, some see it as being an important factor in the transformation of certain villages. In regard to Indonesia, Jean-Luc Maurer writes:

The indirect social impact of tourism in the rural areas of the *DIY* (Daerah Istimewa Yogakarta or Special Territory of Yogyakarta) is not totally negligible. First of all it brings an acceleration of the monetarization process in those villages which are producing handicrafts for the numerous urban based tourist souvenir shops (batik, silver, *wayang kulit,* pottery etc). This monetarization brings, in turn, some change in the villages' social stratification, usually leading towards an increased polarization between a minority of village bureaucrats, self-sufficient land owning farmers, landless peasants and wage-earning laborers or workers on the other hand. Moreover, the development of tourism in the *DIY* indirectly stimulates an already very disturbing rural-urban migration. It creates a whole new range of "pull factors" which combine their effects with traditional "push factors" like landlessness, unemployment and poverty.[52]

Others see tourism as a powerful pressure that can result in the removal of indigenous people from coveted land, especially on the seafront. In Gambia, "Fishermen were banned from beaches allocated to hotel construction and tourist frolics." In Togo, "The construction of the Club Tropicana, begun in 1971, necessitated diverting the international coastal road and burning down the fishing villages of Peda and Fanti, parts of which were reconstructed further East, though at a good distance from the Club."[53] Finally, as J. Bugnicourt notes, we are witnessing, in numerous countries, a real diversion to the profit of tourism of construction and equipment projects that could have benefited the population at large. He cites, for example, the case of the inhabitants of Djerba (an island off Tunisia), where 70 percent of the water distribution goes to hotel consumption, whereas 80 percent of the local people do not have access to water supplies.[54] Two African researchers are in full agreement; "The channeling of resources towards tourist enclaves often deprives the surrounding population of minimum necessities. Thus, drinking water drips out drop by drop in poor suburbs whereas hotel showers, bathrooms, and swimming pools operate at full capacity."[55]

A lot still remains to be said about the cultural effects of tourism, but this is outside the scope of this book. We will round off this theme by quoting from a report on the effect of tourist enclaves owned by Gulf and Western in the Dominican Republic. It was written by the company's Christian shareholders:

> In traveling up and down the tourist centers, we found other tourist social values: the importation of foreign life-styles and tastes, inaccessible to the majority of the local inhabitants; drugs; creation of relations of direct

dependence, including begging; prostitution; support for a black market, especially through the exchange of dollars, which ruins national plans; the creation of groups whose time and energy is devoted to services linked to tourism and activities more connected to fraud and servility than real employment. In the Dominican Republic, tourism is more rowdy, debauched, and elitist than what we have seen elsewhere. There is talk of developing more tourist enclaves, virtually separated from all contact with the country. In some cases there will be direct air links between the resorts and the outside world via private airports.[56]

World of Work

Who has not read advertisements in transnational magazines praising the paradise of assembly industries set up in *economic free zones* (EFZs): "Caribbean Assemblies . . . long term political and economic stability—social progress, education . . . large, urbanized, low-cost labour pool. . . . Long history of labor harmony—strict anti-strike and labor regulation laws." This advertisement, as the name indicates, planned to attract investors towards the Caribbean and more particularly Haiti and the Dominican Republic. It is in the very definition of EFZs that restrictions on workers' rights are found. The South Korean government described some of the characteristics of its zone thus: "The zone has the characteristics of a reserved territory in which the application of laws or relevant regulations is partially or totally suppressed or attenuated. . . . It is an industrial territory in which a series of fiscal and legal privileges are offered to firms of foreign capital (including mixed firms)."[57] Once again it is the Dominican Republic that furnishes the most extreme example of the way these zones can become veritable "regimes of exception." This case has also been the object of the greatest number of studies and denunciations by unions and the American mass media. In 1977 the AFL-CIO accused the EFZ of La Romana (occupied for the most part by firms belonging to Gulf and Western) of paying poverty-level wages and arbitrarily dismissing workers. According to the union report, Gulf and Western "invents its own laws" and "does not allow workers to organize." Once again, the Christian shareholders of Gulf and Western add their own evidence.

> The EFZ is surrounded by barbed wire fences and guarded by soldiers. Some of these measures are necessary to enforce the law, but this system is also destined to prevent the entry of union organizers. . . . The EFZ

of Gulf and Western contributes positively to the development of the Dominican Republic in terms of job creation. However, the capital necessary for the creation of these jobs comes from the efforts of the Dominicans. Many of them would prefer a system that imposed appropriate contributions on companies and allowed workers to organize. The benefits, contributions, and administrative efficiency of Gulf and Western in their job creation programs need to be evaluated in terms of this situation. Gulf and Western's EFZ, such as it presents itself, can simply be envisaged as a temporary transfer of employment from Puerto Rico *en route* for Haiti or another country that pays even less than fifty-five cents an hour. Through its sophisms Gulf and Western lets some progress be envisaged, but this does not obviate the fact that there are some unsolved cases of workers murdered for having tried to attain some dignity, and many other cases of workers who, suffering from hunger, work on silently.[58]

We will come back to the fact that between 70 and 90 percent of the workers in the EFZs are women and that the majority of the industries are devoted to electronics, although items as varied as toys and textiles are also found.

Some have insisted that the presence of these EFZs in Southeast Asia and in countries like Mexico, Haiti, and the Dominican Republic, has fostered the appearance of a worker aristocracy. Speaking of Asia, Marcel Barang sets the record straight: "This is doubtlessly true of the large transnationals, but hardly of the multitude of small, regional firms and joint ventures that today form the bulk of the investors in the EFZs of the poorest countries. Furthermore, the total submission, absence of union rights, and isolation of workers in these zones often represent a loss of ground in relation to the scant gains of the national working class, making social struggles even more difficult. . . . The wages of unskilled or semiskilled workers in Asia are, on average, a tenth of those in the West. Nevertheless, hiring wages of transnational investors are often slightly higher than those of local capitalists; employees have more social advantages and though work relations are more rigid and alienating, they are less feudal than in local capitalists' factories and workshops."[59]

The Uruguayan economist, Raul Trajtenberg, has looked closely at the question of salary differentials: "Various studies show that transnational firms tend to pay slightly higher wages than local firms, though this is truer of American and European transnationals and for skilled workers. Whatever the reason (interfirm competition to obtain the best labor, dissuasion of protest activity, etc.), this difference is minimal in relation to the difference in peripheral and central wages. In Haiti, for example, in 1971, whereas the minimum legal daily wage was $1 (applicable only to the industrial sector), assembly industries paid $1.60 a day. The difference between this and the corresponding wage of $25 in the central countries remained enormous. The raising of the minimum legal wage to $1.30 a day in 1974 scarcely changed the situation."[60] The same author has insisted that low wages are one of the primordial conditions of the investment pattern represented by the EFZ, whose parallel political consequence is the weakness or nonexistence of unions. The figures for work conflicts serve as an indication of this: "If we measure the relation between the number of workers involved in conflicts and the country's active population, the corresponding percentages in South Korea are 0.15 percent between 1965 and 1967, 0.18 percent for 1968–70, and only 0.0002 percent for 1971–73. Other less complete figures indicate that Singapore had a 0.29 percent average for the 1969–74 period and Taiwan, 0.0006 percent for the period 1965–69. The comparable statistics for the United States and Japan for the same decade vary around 3–4 percent."[61] There is a cause for work instability in this apparent climate of social harmony. A spokesman for Mattel (which opened a toy factory in the Mexican EFZ on the border with the United States in the early 1970s) stated that "wages there (Mexicali) have reached parity with other parts of the world, so we can go to other places. We decided we wouldn't reopen the plant permanently. It's all over."[62]

The climate of instability has reached alarming proportions in countries like Hong Kong that drain off an abundance of migrant labor. They employ a good part of the available migrant labour in the region (which includes the Philippines and South Korea, whose skilled workers have been sent to the expanding oil-producing countries of the Middle East, and Singapore, the biggest employer of contract labor, mostly from Malaysia, which makes up 40 percent of its industrial labor force). These regions exhibit a wild capitalism, close to that of nineteenth century Europe. Remarked a study by the Institute of Race Relations:

> Besides the normal situation of the "migrants" familiar to us in Europe, such as the denial of the right to settle or change job without authorization and deportation in the case of unemployment, Singapore forbids migrant workers to marry, except after five years with a dossier "in order" and the authorization of the government, which is given if the couple sign an agreement to be sterilized after their second child. However the lot of indigenous workers in these countries is scarcely better. The price of coffee and a sandwich in a Singapore street is equal to a day's wages. In South Korea girls of twelve or thirteen work eighteen hours a day, seven days

a week, for twelve pounds a month, and Hong Kong is sadly notorious for its exploitation of child labor.[63]

This type of enclave (the first of which dates back to the end of the 1950s) is, owing to the existence of cheap reserves of labor, very different from much older enclaves that owed their existence to the exploitation of natural resources, particularly mines and plantations. The historical analysis of the enclave of the Cerro de Pasco Corporation in Peru by Dirk Kruijt and Menno Vellinga[64] clearly shows how a specific system of domination corresponds with this type of mining enclave (possibility of instant dismissal for personae non gratae; confiscation of their homes and exclusion from the camp; private security police who protect the installations and pressure workers; lockouts, limitation or suppression of the right to organize, hold meetings, or exercise press freedom; transport, if need be, of a large number of strike breakers; use of informers and circulation of a blacklist to all associated companies). What separates the system of domination used in this type of firm from others is the fragmentation it causes in the working population. Here we see a mechanism of superstratification with finer and finer divisions and subdivisions: in 1970 there were 10 functional categories of work, 61 salary scales, 121 duties, and 388 subduties. In this way, as the authors indicate, the division of labour became a control mechanism. The whole system was closer to a caste system than one strictly dividing up the personnel into strata: management, office workers, and other workers were divided from one another by a privilege system (based on salary, quality of living conditions, sources of entertainment, work conditions, proportion of luxury goods, types of schools and teachers, medical and transport services). The clearest result of these policies in Latin American mining enclaves is undoubtedly the fierce opposition of a part of the working class (paid in dollars) to a policy of nationalizing the Chilean copper mines during the Popular Unity government. The National Association of Copper Supervisers and the Confederation of Copper Workers served as a base from 1971 for the regrouping of middle-class associations within the United Federation of Professional Associations. The copper supervisors, as technicians, tried to make their claims common to all professions when they lost their salary in American dollars.[65] To oppose the reforms advocated by Allende, they only had to revitalize this conception dear to the transnational firms that employed them: the union had the character of a corporation, contrasting strongly to other unions issued from the historic struggles of the Chilean workers' movement.

The union that has been bought up by employers' ideas on the natural harmony between capital and labor will always remain a temptation for the transnational firm grappling with workers' demands. As recently as July 1980, Coca-Cola threatened its 4,250 workers in Mexico, already on strike for a month, with dismissal, while installing a scab union; all this as a response to the workers' demand for a revision of their contract.[66] Outside these territories of exception that enclaves constitute, the attitude of transnational firms in respect to working-class organizations depends on the nature and room for manoeuvering of workers' movements in each country, as well as the balance of power between social partners. Sometimes, but very rarely, the mechanisms of international solidarity have an influence.

The still hotly-debated case of Coca-Cola Guatemala is as revealing of the repugnance felt by transnationals in having to negotiate on a multinational basis with unions as it is of new forms of union resistance. In this case, the owner of the Coca-Cola franchise in Guatemala had refused its workers the right to organise. Since 1978, twelve workers, including several union officials, have been killed trying to obtain recognition of a union as the representative of some four hundred workers. To forward their cause, this union contacted the International Union of Food and Allied Workers Associations (IUF), whose affiliates organized boycotts and demonstrations against Coca-Cola throughout the world in thirty countries. Not wanting a human rights issue on its hands, Coca-Cola arranged to cede the franchise to a new owner. At the same time, a real union, whose officials were protected against being dismissed and which had a notice board at its disposal, was recognised. This final victory, accompanied by the reinstatement of all unjustly dismissed workers, was, as is evidenced by an exchange of telegrams, the fruit of negotiation between Coca-Cola and the IUF. *Business Week* (November 24, 1980) reported that "Coke now denies that the boycotts had any effect . . . Coke denies that it negotiated with the IUF; Coke says that its representatives met with IUF officials merely to keep them abreast of the company's effort to find a new franchise owner, and notes that it did not negotiate a labor contract."

This is obviously not the opinion of the IUF officials nor of the director of the Wharton School's Industrial Research Unit who, "for years, has closely monitored all 'contacts' between labour federations and corporations and is an outspoken critic of union efforts to bargain accross national boundaries," and who stated, "It would appear that Coca-Cola's lack of preparation and understanding of the nature of relationships led it into a virtual de facto recognition of the IUF. They gave the IUF a big political victory." Hoping to avoid a precedent, Coca-Cola thought it wise to send to all its branches, notably its franchise branches, the same denial it sent to all the major newspapers. In *Le Monde* (February 7, 1982) Coca-Cola reiterated that "it had not taken part in negotiations."

A final reference, this time to the executive employment policies of transnational firms. Our example comes from Morocco and concerns a policy that distinguishes between nationals and expatriates. It opposes giving positions of responsibility to nationals (key posts like managing director, financial director, and technical director). Once again, the policy of European (particularly French) TFs is very different from that of subsidiaries of American transnationals. The former have generally agreed to "Moroccanize" key posts, whereas firms like Goodyear, General Tire, and Proctor and Gamble have not done so. The case of IBM is different, doubtlessly because IBM-Morocco is a branch of IBM-France. To compensate for this lack of delegation of responsibility, higher salaries are granted to nationals. These salaries serve as reference points for the establishment of salaries (whether ratified by the government or not) for private and public duties. In a country like Morocco, characterized by a shortage of executives, this is typical enough. As Bachir Hamdouch reported in 1980, "At the time of the official 'Moroccanization' policy, the risks of a hemorrhage of executives from the public sector towards the private were such that the state was induced to increase salaries substantially in one way or another. This osmosis in executives' remuneration widened the gap between higher and lower salaries, thus running counter to the official incomes policy initiated by the government in the last few years aiming at the increase of lower salaries in order to reduce social disparity."[67]

Role of Women

Between 80 and 90 percent of the assembly industry's labor force are women. In the electronics industry, 85 percent of the staff are women, and men are only found in jobs requiring an engineering diploma and at the management level as foremen, personnel managers, and works managers. Young men working in electronics factories are usually employed as storemen.

Many transnational officials maintain that work and the fact of getting out of the house introduce a radical rupture in the subordinate status of women. Paradoxically enough, this quality of subordination is sought after by transnationals to assure a passive, tranquil work force, both the EFZs and elsewhere. "A man just won't stay in this tedious kind of work. He'd walk out in a couple of hours," said a young American manager who was recruiting staff for a factory in Ciudad Juárez, Mexico. The personnel manager of a light assembly plant in Taiwan told the anthropologist Linda Gail Arrigo: "Young male workers are too restless and impatient to do monotonous work with no career value. If displeased, they sabotage the machines and even threaten the foreman. But girls? At most, they cry a little."[68] Even if certain forms of protest are permitted, they are still referred to traditional images of women: hysteria is somewhat less dangerous than unions, and spirit possession is the only cultural outlet for woman workers. Thus in Malaysia, as a study in the *Southeast Asia Chronicle* expressed it: "Without strikes, without unions, without collective bargaining, apparitions of 'spirits' affecting hundreds of women workers has led to the closing of factories, sometimes for hours, sometimes for days on end. Spirits give discomfited women one of the rare culturally acceptable forms of social protest. . . . These phenomena of possession generally occur during tense periods due to intense production or changes in production methods. . . . To put an end to these collective crises, managers went to the trouble of bringing in public relations experts from New York or hiring a sorcerer for a month to exorcise the 'spirits,' but the possessions continued."[69]

When the managers of Mexican-border plants realized during the first strike involving women that they were no longer "easily governable and disciplined" beings who had never ceased showing "a spirit of loyalty towards their companies," they complained of people "who put on a front of being simple peasants, but they know what the hell they are doing."[70]

Union action is more than ever considered as the formidable enemy and women are scared to organize themselves. This is illustrated by a woman Gulf and Western worker in the Dominican Republic: "We once tried to start a union, but a lot of people lost their jobs; they are no longer allowed to enter the duty-free zone, as they have been banned. Here we say nothing, absolutely nothing against the company. Some women would; but the majority are scared, especially those with a lot of children. These women say, 'I don't want to have anything to do with it because they will sack me.' "[71] When something is done in countries with tough regimes like Guatemala, as in 1975 in a North American jeans factory, the American managers called in the local police under the pretext that the strikers were "under the thumb of communists."[72]

Two American anthropologists have analysed particularly well how the subordinate status of women resists being changed when it is integrated into the world of work: There are structural limits to the extent to which the development of capitalism decomposes the forms of womens' subordination, so that the overall effect is the transformation of womens' subordination rather than its dissolution. The extent to which women becoming wage earners decomposes the form of womens' subordination depends principally on how large the wage is; how regular and secure the employment is; the extent to which the wage-earner has control over the spending of the wage; and the extent to which the capitalist form of social production is compatible with the responsibilities of bringing up children. The lower the wage, the more unstable the employment, and the less control which the wage earner has over the spending of the wage, the less likely is wage work to free women from pre-capitalist forms of dependence on men. The type of employment offered in the industries we are considering is not, and does not seem likely to become, high wage high security employment.[73]

The work conditions in Gulf and Western's EFZs in the Dominican Republic, described by the AFL-CIO as a "modern slave labor camp," are similar. Firstly, the forms of surveillance are invested with all the violence of macho culture. "In the factories there are controllers whose job is to make women work, watch them to make sure they don't talk, and see what they do. They do not allow us any breathing space. They are completely arbitrary, swear, and treat us like animals. I've even seen them slapping women and screaming at them in filthy language to get out."[74] Instability is another form of control. "They hire women and sack them after three months so that they have no rights. They return after two or three months and are sometimes rehired, though in three months, it's the same thing all over again."[75] According to American standards, the electronics industry is a high risk one because of the use of a number of highly toxic substances. Many studies have been carried out to measure the effect of the use of acid on workers. Some results were reported in the magazine *Ms* in January 1981:

> In one stage of the electronics assembly process, the workers have to dip the circuits into open vats of acid. According to Irene Johnson and Carol Bragg, who toured the National Semiconductor plant in Penang, Malaysia, the women who do the dipping "wear rubber gloves and boots, but these sometimes leak, and burns are common." Occasionally whole fingers are lost. More commonly, what electronics workers lose is the 20/20 vision they are required to have when they are hired. Most electronics workers spend seven to nine hours a day peering through microscopes, straining to meet their quota. One study in South Korea found that most electronics assembly workers developed severe eye problems after only one year of employment: 88 percent had chronic conjunctivitis; 44 percent became

nearsighted; and 19 percent developed astigmatism. A manager from Hewlett-Packard's Malaysia plant, in an interview with Rachel Grossman, denied that there were any eye problems: "These girls are used to working with 'scopes. We've found no eye problems. But it sure makes me dizzy to look through those things."[76]

The majority of existing studies on the place of women in transnational industries have taken work in the EFZs as their field of observation, particularly the electronics industries. There are very few studies, on the other hand, on the work of women in transnational subsidiaries of, for example, agribusiness. Ernest Feder's study on imperialism in the strawberry industry in Mexico reinforces through its observations on the work of women in this sector the arguments we have just made. The supervisors were women, though no less ferocious: "Practically all the workers were extremely reluctant to discuss work conditions and were terrified at the thought that a revelation might lead to them being sacked. Probably the women who despotically watch over them had warned them not to talk with foreigners. In a busy season, women work eighteen to nineteen hours in a row with only small breaks. . . . These conditions lead to a deterioration in their health and nervous tension in an essentially hypermonotonous activity, requiring no qualifications whatsoever."[77]

The concept of women underlying the work conditons of millions of young women in the periphery is in violent contrast with the concept advanced by transnational culture industries. It is in contrast with the image of the modern woman as the symbol of modernity, center of the world of consumption, which is proposed to all women as an ideal. It is in their conception of women that the homogenizing and universalizing strategy of the transnational media can be caught in the act of creating the illusion of a world free of class contradictions.[78]

4
Regulatory Efforts and Policies

Throughout the numerous and varied fields of observation that make up the analysis in the two preceding chapters, a model of development imposed on Third World societies can be extricated. In this model the road to progress passes through integration into the transnational system. It is in this state of subordination that the developing countries are inserted into the world economy. In the introduction, I situated critically the notion of dependence, pointing out that if it was true that developing countries occupied a subordinate place in relation to the central countries that control the international economic system, it was no less true that each region, each situation has its own particular mode of integration into this "modern world system," which is no more than a "single market," to use the term of E. Wallerstein and *Business Week*. There are, in effect, numerous modes of subordination of local bourgeoisies to transnational capital. I have insisted that, to deepen our knowledge of this notion of dependence and subordination, we must increasingly examine the nature of the dominant classes in each social formation. As Gonzalo Arroyo, speaking of the "dependent" bourgeoisies of Latin America and refusing to equate *dependence* with *passivity,* remarked: "They have participated actively or passively in the setting up of authoritarian or even military governments, which have replaced liberal democracies in some South American countries. However, today they are actively seeking to fit into the international market, implying a profound social and economic restructuring in several countries. Let us make no mistake; this bourgeoisie is not only likely to create in certain cases an economic dynamism (in spite of the structural contradictions) but also an ideological domination, based on free enterprise, economic individualism, and consumerism, the natural ally of national security and anti-Communism, linked to the thesis that all politics are corrupt."[1]

These comments are particularly important for situating the efforts of developing countries to counterbalance or halt the socio-cultural impact of transnational firms; if it is more and more true, as even the transnationals themselves affirm, that we are witnessing a "nationalism" that inspires all Third World countries seeking regulatory mechanisms for transnational investments, it is even more true that under this umbrella of nationalism, very different political regimes with extremely diverse roads of development often take shelter. Some basically seek to renegotiate their participation in the peripheral capitalist system, that is, get their share of the cake in a world system whose structures remain profoundly marked by unequal exchange, whereas others try to question this state of subordination implied in the capitalist system of production and consumption and escape from its orbit. Still others try to combine both positions and blessed with natural resources, try to affirm their position as preferential partners in a relationship more advantageous, but still subordinated to the center. In this case, not only the project of the national dominant class for the exploitation of local resources but also the projects of the other classes play a part. This elementary distinction prevents us putting on the same level, for example, measures for regulating advertising agencies in countries marked by strongman regimes, and the overall restructuring of national communications systems by countries applying to the letter the doctrine of self-reliance. At a time when, according to the transnationals' own diagnosis, "Developing nations have grown more sophisticated in controlling foreign-owned enterprises" and "More and more developing countries are requiring that foreign investors maximize their use of local content in manufacturing, that they increase local processing, or that they meet certain export goals"[2] through government intervention policies in developing countries, a whole range of positions that face up to their structural dependence are unveiled. The terms *cultural identity, national sovereignty, nationalism* and *nationalisation* can give rise to many interpretations. In 1970, I wrote about Chile: "It goes without saying that it is not simply by suppressing all programmes manufactured abroad—especially those from North America—that the degree of cultural dependency will be reduced. A 'Chileanised' programme can reproduce exactly the same ideology and therefore be guilty of the same vices as foreign material, the only difference being that these vices may perhaps be less explicit."[3]

In the introduction and the first two chapters, I have tried to demonstrate how the transnational cultural and social networks can only be explained by a model of development. These networks are the nonmaterial and material transmission belts of this model of production and consumption, as much ways of integration into the economy as into the attitudes of the consumer, citizen, and producer that this economy needs. This implies refusing the myth of "free choice" as a model of development, a myth that confuses the freedom of capital with freedom, and rejecting theoreticians like Brezinski who celebrate "the end of imperialism" in the ecumenism of the "communications revolution" and the techno-scientific revolution.

It is in light of this general truth that the different responses offered by various societies of the periphery and within these societies by different social sectors to the penetration of colonizing cultural models, must be evaluated. The cultural networks of integration into the center are also premises for the integration into an economic and political system; that is, they prepare, maintain, reproduce, and adapt this integration in a dialectical exchange. Here, the term, *process,* synonymous with movement, takes its real meaning.

In this fourth chapter, the different objectives, measures, policies, and strategies adopted by the peripheral countries' authorities to redress, correct, or eliminate the negative effects of transnationals, will be reviewed. Nothing could be more difficult than to set out these governmental experiences and draw theoretical lessons from them with a view to developing policies, as one must be careful to avoid an ahistorical conception of these policies and to take into account the whole context that nourishes them.

Advertising Codes and Regulations

Foreign Languages, Materials, and Ownership

In 1979 an in-depth survey by J.J. Boddewyn, sponsored by the International Advertising Association, covering thirty-five countries, drew up a balance sheet of the regulations imposed by various countries on foreign advertisements. A number of countries have ad hoc regulations, although their content and spirit are often different. Although affirming that "liberalism generally prevails in most countries regarding advertising restrictions," the report observed that "there is increasing pressure towards greater restrictions in Australia, Colombia, France, Malaysia, Quebec province, Venezuela and Mexico, many of which may be termed 'pilot' countries, imitated by others in their region."[4] The transnational language, English more often than not, is banned in several countries where it is not the common language, and advertising material must be produced in the country. The above study underlines the extreme case of Peru, "the most restrictive of the most restrictive": "No foreign-language periodicals published in Peru can carry foreign-language ads. No advertising materials such as commercials to be shown in Peru can be produced abroad. Only Peruvian residents can take part in advertising produced in Peru. If an advertiser still believes that a foreign language or materials can enhance his sales pitch to Peruvians, his only outlet is direct mail."[5] In Peru, as well as in Mexico, the brand names of foreign companies must be translated into the local language or be bilingual "under certain conditions." Trying to explain the reason behind these measures, the IAA report compared the principal motives pushing industrialized countries to exercise linguistic control over advertising in developing countries:

> In non-western countries, motivating factors are nationalistic and cultural in orientation—whether to remove the stigma of colonialism, to forge a new common national or regional identity, or merely to resist the anglicisation of the local language. For example, Peruvian regulations stress the protection and enhancement of the national culture and of the "Peruvian man" and therefore try to ban foreign-inspired models and materials. The Philippine government urges the use of the Tagalog language to express that country's "independence from foreigners." Similar measures have been taken in Malaysia, which favors, "a major native language at the expense of English and of minority languages such as Chinese and Tamil."

Thailand in 1979 promoted within the framework of the Consumer Protection Act approved by the Thai government new regulations for advertising, trade labels, and warranties. Articles of these guidelines disapprove "texts that may cause disunity among the people," or "that directly or indirectly support a legal or moral offense," or are "detrimental to the national culture." These texts have led to accusations that their instigators have promoted "arbitrary rulings."[6]

The decision of several governments to reduce foreign control over advertising agencies is in the same spirit. In the Andean pact countries, for example (Venezuela, Colombia, Ecuador, and Peru), foreign advertising agencies can only be 19 percent foreign owned. We have already pointed out the cases of India and Nigeria, where advertising agencies have come under "indigenization" decrees, which affect the majority of industrial sectors as well. The previously quoted reflection of a representative of the Nigerian subsidiary of a transnational agency showed that, in default of ownership, there were other ways of maintaining contact with the transnational network and bypassing the obstacles put up by "indigenization." Similarly in the Andean pact countries, where, as recently as August 1980, *Advertising Age* September 8, 1980 reported: "Grey Advertising completed an exclusive affiliation agreement with Compania Nacional de Publicidad in Peru. Several other agencies are trying to set up similar affiliation agreements in Peru and in other Andean Pact countries, like Ecuador and Colombia, which impose heavy penalties on or bar outright foreign ownership of ad agencies."

The problem is obvious. The measures we have just mentioned are often no more than the threshold of a policy of regulation. The most difficult task remains to be done. The case of Venezuela clearly illustrates the difficulties that peripheral countries have to face when they decide to transform the orientation of their advertising systems and alleviate or suppress the pressure it exercises on the whole of the mass communications system. The excessive size of the advertising system and its weight on the press, radio, and television has already been pointed out as one of the major characteristics of the Venezuelan communications system. More than ever in Venezuela, "Advertising is the vertebral column not only of the private radio-broadcasting system . . . but the whole mass culture."[7] This strength of advertising power contrasts heavily with the weakness of existing legislation regulating advertisements. In 1976 the drafters of the RATELVE project, whose goal was to propose a new radio-television broadcasting policy for the Venezuelan state, asserted: "For twenty-five years, while the media attained the absolute power they now enjoy, manipulated by advertisers and advertising people, for the most part, foreign, the Venezuelan state has only made two innocuous, reiterative provisions, aimed at regulating minor, marginal forms of advertising. . . . In fact, the state has not only sinned through omission and permissiveness, but has frankly supported the private sector."[8] One of the regulations to which the authors refer, enacted in November 1972, was concerned with the regulation of advertising for alcohol and cigarettes during children's programs. The RATELVE project also noted that the power of advertisers and advertising people was exorbitant, as they violated the feeble existing laws and replaced them with their own. As Osvaldo Capriles wrote in 1976, "The regulations have been held up for ridicule in the most brazen, insolent manner possible by private enterprises. The advertising regulations are openly transgressed as is the obligation to reserve a percentage of space for education and public information by state organs. In 1968 the private sector agreed on advertising percentages scandalously exceeding the limits established in the regulations of one minute or 150 words of advertising between programs; the convention of the private sector brazenly increased these commercial interuptions to a maximum of four minutes, that is, the private sector *made legislation* in its own interest by exceeding the existing ordinance."[9] This power of advertising was concretized from 1970 on by the creation of the *Consejo Venezolano de la Publicidad,* which regrouped the Venezuelan television, cinema, radio, and press federations as well as the Venezuelan Federation of Advertising Agencies (FEVAP) and the Venezuelan Association of Advertisers (ANDA). Of the seventy-eight members of ANDA, forty-eight were foreign firms. The virulence of the private sector's reaction to the RATELVE project was equal to the damage that a minimum planning of communication would do to their interests.

In 1980 the sixth Venezuelan national development plan included a plan for the social communication sector. There, we can find principles establishing the idea of the need for planning in this sector in a perspective of "endogenous cultural development."[10] After having noted that media messages have a regressive effect on the reinforcement of national identity, this plan asserted the following:

> The recent experience of the Venezuelan state as regards the planning of social communication has not allowed for the linking of this communication to the requirements of national development. In this sense, the nonexistence of an integrated framework of communication policy allowing the orientation and coordination of diverse institutional efforts carried out in several basic sectors of development constitutes a critical component tending to becoming more and more serious. Moreover, it must be pointed out that no real legislation exists as regards communication, in keeping with its importance. This juridicial anachronism leaves the state stranded and without the means that allow it to accomplish its role of agent of planning, regulation, and instigation of specific initiatives in this domain.

The plan proposes a series of measures destined to establish what it calls "a new national order of information and communication" for the period 1980–85. Its principal merit is to have reformulated the policy of various means of communication owned by the state in the direction of an opening towards all social groups and linking these means to priority development sectors. However, as two researchers of ININCO (from the Central University of Venezuela) remark, one of the most acknowledged weaknesses of the plan is that the measures suggested affect exclusively the public sector. They note that if it is important to reorientate advertising investments and public information in the public sector in fulfillment of this endogenous policy of national identity (like Mexico, the Venezuelan state has a very high advertising budget and advertises heavily in the commercial media), one can only speak of a new national order of information and communication if this new order takes in the means and systems of communication of the private sector as well.[11] The case of Venezuela is worth following, as among developing countries it is undoubtedly the one where the idea of communication planning is the most evolved, even if the results, because of numerous interests still at work and the immense development reached by the advertising sector, do not always conform to official principles. It is, for example, one of the few countries of the Third World to accommodate in one of its universities a training center specialized in the planning of cultural and communication processes.

Consumer Protection

It is undoubtedly about the promotion and selling of milk powder for children that the most important initiatives for the promotion of a code of ethics have been crystalized. The adoption by some transnational companies of a common or individual code is the best proof of this. However, let us listen to Pierre Borgoltz on the efficiency of these codes. Although recognizing that the codes of conduct elaborated by the industry and adopted on a voluntary basis may constitute a first step towards the reform of the promotion of infant formula in LDCs, he notes:

> If the companies have come to recognise publicly that their previous promotion activities needed to be revised, their response falls generally short of a significant reconsideration of the way in which they conduct business and promote formula products. The restraints on promotion that have been adopted in the different "codes of ethics" are actually of such modest consequences that they appear more aimed at defusing public criticism rather than evolving from a serious self-questioning of the legitimacy of their promotion activities in LDCs.
>
> In particular, the "code of ethics" adopted by the members of the International Council of the Infant Food Industry has been criticised for this reason. It is setting restraints for instance on what types of uniforms the mothercraft personnel should wear, when it is the existence of such sales personnel itself that is questionable, let alone its masquerading. In the same spirit, companies' recognition of the superiority of mother's milk

has been in fact transformed into yet another commercial appeal for the formula products.[12]

He goes so far as to suggest that these voluntary codes, according to available information, will be short-lived and will doubtless follow the descending curve followed by the voluntary codes adopted by the nine big companies of the U.S. cigarette industry which, five years later, were to be observed by only two of them.

After the translation of the book *The Baby Killer* into three local languages and thanks to the growing preoccupation of local pediatricians and nutritionists, and the dramatic increase of breast-feeding groups, Malaysia promulgated an ethical code in June 1979, where one can read among its sixteen points, "The use of media is inappropriate to sales promotional messages for infant formula products." Also forbidden were promotional messages aimed at consumers like "with packet offers, redemption schemes, free gifts unrelated to purchases and temporary price-off offers."[13] Also attacking an extremely widespread form of direct contact with the consumer called the "baby show," a sort of beauty contest for babies, the Malaysian code of ethics stipulated, "Companies marketing infant formula products are not to be associated in any manner with baby shows."

Countries like Singapore, Indonesia, Nigeria, and the Philippines have adopted similar codes. The need for such codes, promoted by local governments, has been stressed by Pierre Borgoltz, who writes: "Government regulations seem necessary to avoid any degeneration of the voluntary codes and incentives to circumvent them. Because when this happens, even for a single company, then there is necessarily an escalation from the other companies and the policing effect vanishes quickly. So far, companies appear to have a hard time complying with the codes they have themselves devised. The existence of binding regulations facilitates the companies' observance of principles they may value, but which the dynamics of competitive promotion undermine."[14]

This is one of the major preoccupations running through the "Draft International Code of Marketing of Breastmilk Substitutes," proposed in December 1980 by WHO, which takes up, although filing off somewhat the aggressive rough edges, some already-promoted local codes, notably advising that, "marketing personnel, in their business capacity, shall not seek direct or indirect contact of any kind with pregnant women or with mothers of infants and young children." In Article 4, it insisted that "governments shall have the responsibility to ensure that objectives and consistent information is provided on infants and young children for use by families and those involved in the field of infant and child nutrition. This responsibility shall cover either the planning, provision, design and dissemination of information, or their control."

Outside the strict domain of infant feeding, regulations on promotion and marketing are rarer. This is the conclusion arrived at by Charles Medawar, who notes that very few countries have adopted national legislation on advertising, tending in the same direction. In 1974, the report of Gaedeke and Udo-Aka suggested that six out of ten developing countries had no specific legislation protecting the consumer. Among the reasons invoked, we find expressed in the answers of several diplomats the idea that, "the government is still in an early stage of development and is devoting its energies and concern to more important domestic problems. We do not have technical and administrative capabilities to handle such a difficult, though important, task as consumer protection."[15] Or again: "your questions with regard to quality, safety, product warranties etc seem to be unrelated to the realities of (the) present day . . . the questions will undoubtedly assume importance as the country progresses toward a modern monetary economy, when consumer tastes and the need [for] greater protection will be vital elements of the overall economic policy."[16]

However, there do exist international codes either already clarified or in the course of elaboration, formulated either by the International Chamber of Commerce (1975) or international organisations of the UN like the Center on Transnational Corporations.[17] In October 1980, the commission on transnational corporations brought together the Intergovernmental Working Group in Geneva to discuss a draft report on codes of conduct. Four articles on consumer protection defined its field of application, whereas three others defined how the protection of the environment could be widened. Necessarily of a general character, they nevertheless constitute an important declaration of principles and could play the same role as the code put out by WHO to which we have referred. Let us quote the second article:

> Transnational corporations shall/should, in respect of the products and services which they produce or market, or propose to produce or market in any country, supply to the competent authorities of that country on request, or on a regular basis as specified by these authorities, all relevant information concerning:
> —characteristics of these products or services which may be injurious to the health and safety of consumers including experimental uses and related aspects;

—prohibitions, restrictions, warnings and other public regulatory measures imposed in other countries on grounds of health and safety protection on these products or services.[18]

The draft, approved unanimously by the thirty-member executive board of the World Health Organisation in January 1981, was adopted by 100 to 1 (the United States) with 9 abstentions in May 1981 at the World Health Assembly in Geneva. During this assembly the opposition of the United States, based on the fact that the code was "contrary to the principle of free enterprise that President Reagan's government had promised to defend," was felt once again.

In the food sector, along with measures that impose, for example, a minimum proportion of local raw materials in manufacture, several countries have taken a series of measures in the packaged foods sector, concerning controls over trademarks, advertising, and marketing practices. As for the use of foreign trademarks, countries like Mexico have gone as far as to stipulate that "both trademarks (foreign and national) must be used in an equally prominent way." As a study by the CTC remarked:

> By initiating a parallel national trademark system, developing countries are presumably seeking to segregate consumers' concern with quality control from the advantages enjoyed by TNCs from aggressive promotion of their brand-names, and thus to reduce the competitive position of such products. In so far as national trademarks substantially increase local competition and efficiency, they may be expected to improve availabilities of lower-cost foods. Some countries, like Zambia for example, have preferred to channel through public agencies or non-commercial circuits products available under generic names at lower prices than the differentiated products.[19]

As I have already noted several times, the most important groups likely to exercise pressure on various governments and on transnationals themselves are national and international consumer organisations or public interest groups not only in the denunciation of exactions or excesses but also in the assistance of local communities and educational programs. The methods of action on the local level of one of these groups, the Consumers' Association of Penang (Malaysia), was the subject of an in-depth study by Khor Kok Peng, published in July–August 1980. Summarizing one of the educational programs that CAP launched in fifty schools and in several areas, the author writes: "Through the Education Programme, CAP aims to battle the insidious influence of the consumer culture. Young students discover the nutritional bankruptcy of junk food and soft drinks, misleading advertisements, dangerous drugs and food additives. Workers become conscious of hazards in the working place and the effect of inflation in their take-home pay. Housewives and working women learn about dangerous cosmetics and contraceptives, the irrationality of falling prey to fashion and the value of breast-feeding. The Programme is carried out through talks, slide shows, films, discussions, workshops, exhibitions and joint surveys with the various groups."[20]

The regulation of the promotion of pharmaceutical products presupposes a series of steps that only a few countries have begun to undertake very recently. The need to adopt a restricted and rationalized list of essential drugs to fight against the proliferation and excessive competition of brands has been to the forefront of discussion not only at WHO but also at UNCTAD, for example. Several governments like Brazil, India, and Sri Lanka have already proposed for some time the introduction of restricted lists of medicines that according to organizations like WHO or UNIDO should not exceed 200–300. In India a government committee has estimated that of the 15,000 medicines and drugs currently on sale in the country, only 116 were essential.[21] As Lall and Bibile remarked in 1978 in their study, *Medicine for the year 2000,* two powerful forces are likely to hamper the introduction of these restricted lists: the drug industry both locally and foreign-owned and the medical profession. This explains the compromise instituted in a country like Brazil between the free market and the restricted list. The latter is only applied in a limited market, for example, among the impoverished classes of the Northeast. The second policy option, which also prepares for the adoption of a distribution of medicines not confided to advertising laws, has been carried out with mixed success in various countries with a goal to satisfying their medical needs in the most economical way possible; it consists in the rationalization and centralization of the buying on a national or regional scale of medicines to be sold under their generic names.

A third option is to begin the construction of one's own pharmaceutical industry by getting into one or another of the three levels of the process: dosage formulation and packaging, production based on intermediates, production based on raw materials. The first requires only a relatively simple technology, available in numerous Third World countries. The other two are much more complex. "If a country decides to produce drugs domestically, it can adopt two parallel strategies: (1) it can integrate backwards—that is, gradually increase the level of sophistication starting from packaging, working up gradually to dosage formulation, and finally engaging in the production of bulk medicinals; and (2) it can gradually switch the control of domestic production facilities from TNCs to the control of local industry. Whichever route a country decides on, it always will have to consider the problems related to the protection of the local industry, adequate standards of quality, and the necessary technology."[22]

It is undoubtedly this complexity that explains why very few Third World countries have even the embryonic form of a real local pharmaceutical industry at their disposal.

These options obviously challenge systems of market promotion and induce the finding of other means of access to the consumer. This is suggested by the study of Chakravarthi Raghavan.

> Health service schemes and the drugs distribution system should be modified to ensure supply to the entire population. Countries should consider adopting a multi-tier system: a special cadre of para-medical personnel at different local levels working in cooperation with general physicians and specialists at the referral and specialist hospitals.
>
> Unconventional methods of delivery of essential drugs could be explored, using rural school teachers, postmasters or a group of trained special rural pharmacists. Many countries in the 1930s did this to provide quinine to tackle malaria.[23]

Food Self-Reliance and the Advertising System

In order to face up to the malnutrition of the majority of the population, the Mexican government has developed a strategy for producing basic foods and establishing consumption targets for these foods. The goal of this strategy (SAM-Sistema Alimentario Mexicano) is to reach a production of basic food allowing for self-sufficiency in the agricultural sector as well as in fishing. The SAM project not only pursues an objective of social justice (an adequate and endogenous production of working-class foods, which helps to redistribute revenues) but also aims at economic sovereignty. For in order to be able to reorientate the consumption of the vast majority towards the satisfaction of the minimum needs of well-being by producing and producing basic foods on a large scale, the total reorganisation of agriculture, the dynamization of the fishing industry, and the extension of the internal market needs to take place. Also needed is the creation of rural employment and a better distribution of revenues. It is also a response to the needs of national sovereignty. The SAM project even speaks of the food question conceived of in terms of self-sufficiency, as a question of "security"; food "security" is defined as "the possibility of continued access in time and space to essential foods for the development and normal functioning of individuals in society." In the presentation of the 1980–82 plan, we read: "If we do not want to reduce to nothing the exceptional and transitory advantages of our favorable energy position, it is indispensable to formulate a policy of self-sufficiency for basic foods, especially cereals and oil-producing plants. It is obviously not a question of considering self-sufficiency as an obstinate, costly autarky. It does not run counter to our exportation of fruits and early produce. We simply state that Mexico, unlike the majority of Third World countries, has an extraordinary potential to be self-sufficient in grains, without penalising the production of other goods. . . . Foods will continue daily to be increasingly used as strategic elements of negotiation and even pressure."[24] The SAM project insists particularly on the vulnerability of developing countries' economies. In 1985 it is estimated that these countries will have a grain deficit nearly double that of 1980:85 million metric tons. Five or six firms, the majority of which are North American, control around 85 percent of the world grain market. Over the last five years, the price of cereals and oil-producing plants has increased more than that of manufactured goods and even oil itself. The SAM project is finally a response to the model that transfers the production and consumption from advanced countries to poor countries.

A preferential target population is therefore defined: in 1979, 13 million in rural zones and 6 million in urban zones. The total target population is about 35 million Mexicans, that is, all those who do not reach the minimum nutritional norm of 2,750 calories and eighty grams of protein. The preferential target population is defined as those with an extremely low nutritional level. A recommended basic shopping basket of foods was drawn up. Its structure and content are the real expression of nutritional needs of the national population as much as the target-population and takes into account regional consumption habits and purchasing capacity. This basic shopping basket fulfills five fundamental conditions: it reaches the normative nutritional minimum and considers the production cost of primary materials that have an effect on the final price of foods; it takes into account the purchasing power of the population as well as national and regional consumption habits; finally, it considers the potential of the country in terms of human and natural resources in the agricultural and food sectors as well as the fish industry. On the basis of resources available in different regions, three types of recommended shopping basket were drawn up. In the North, emphasis was placed on wheat; in the gulf zone, on rice; and in the Southeast, on corn. Everywhere, the need to complement this diet with beans was insisted on. The basic shopping basket becomes thus an instrument for state economic planning for self-sufficiency as it links necessities with production possibilities. However, at the same time, it is also a questioning of the various channels of commercialization. In this food stategy, promotion and education occupy a prime place.

> To produce and distribute the foods of the basic recommended shopping basket in quantity with a quality and price that is adequate to the consumers' requirements is not enough. On top of this, the consumers need to identify the satisfaction of their food needs with these products, which is currently not the case, following the effect of commercial advertising that has imposed impoverished distortions on national food habits from which low-income sectors have not escaped. . . . This makes a permanent campaign with commercial broadcasting means necessary in order to rectify the consumption patterns imposed by the transnational food industry for the most part and to succeed in incorporating the recommended basic shopping basket into the normal diet of our target population.

The different channels of this food promotion and education are commercial radio and television, the rural television system, rural and urban schools, and, particularly important, free school textbooks. It is obviously too soon to evaluate the impact of this strategy on the Mexican food system, which has recently increased dramatically. As in any project of this scope, the clash of interests can cause antagonism between different sectors of economic and political power. However, one thing is certain: the SAM project has stimulated creative reflection on the development of plans conceived within the perspective of self-reliance.

It contributes decisively, in particular, to the domain of reflection on a self-reliant use of mass-communication means. Two fundamental recommendations can be extricated: the need to observe the legislation already in force and the need to carry out reforms as quickly as possible, at the very least for food and alcohol advertising. It is urgent to restrict the promotion of alcohol, costly foods with little nutritional value, and tobacco. However, the role played by the means of communication does not end there, for the production strategy of SAM requires not only a transformation of producer and consumer behavior but also a progressive change of the technologies that allow a greater productivity of basic foods. It is thus a massive program of promotion and education to make understood through means of private and state broadcasting and direct communication the need to improve the general conditions of production, as well as the advantages of the recommended shopping basket of basic foods. Two programs catered to this promotion and education. First, the national program of nutritional promotion and education showed ways of complementing foods for children and pregnant mothers, instilling hygiene and health habits. It also pointed out ways of cultivating gardens and fish farms, thanks to rural animators relayed across the country through mass communications. Second, the SAM project proposed a broadcast campaign directed at the mother-child unit to promote the virtues of traditional Mexican family cooking. The goal of the second program, the National Program of Orientation and Support for Agricultural Production and Productivity, is to supply information for a technological organization and orientation (for example, information on credit quotas assigned to each type of cultivation, transport mechanisms, commercialisation, etc.). Under this heading, the contributions of research institutes are considered as well as a recollection of traditional peasant practices that have proved their validity in agricultural output and intensive use of the soil. The study underway of the UN Research Institute for Social Development (UNRISD), which also insists on food security, should contribute numerous elements for judging these strategies against hunger and isolating the different factors that make the development programs of many poor countries favor the production of luxury foods or nonfood agricultural products, destined mainly for exportation, instead of the production of basic foods. Through the approach it advocates to the food problem, an approach not considered exclusively as a technological problem requiring technical solutions, this study should help, above all, to bring out the way in which essential relations of structures work within food systems and which, as in any other social system, are largely determined by the balance of power between often antagonistic social forces at the local, national, or international level.

New International Information Order

Parallel with the demand for a New International Economic Order is the demand for a New International Information Order (NIIO). Numerous conferences have stressed the need for the machinery to implement this order. Under the auspices of organizations like UNESCO and, in particular, the

Nonaligned Movement, conferences have been held at Algiers, 1973; Lima, 1975; Mexico City, 1976; New Delhi, 1976; Colombo, 1976; San José (Costa Rica), 1976; Nairobi, 1976; Lomé, 1979; Kuala Lumpur, 1979; and the General Conference of UNESCO in Belgrade at the end of 1980, where the MacBride report on the problems of communication was approved. The goal of the NIIO is to reequilibrate an international flow of information marked by unequal exchange.

The main activity to date has been concentrated on the creation of national agencies or networks of information agencies in peripheral countries. In 1980 the pool of the nonaligned countries' news agencies, founded in 1975 on the initiative of the Yugoslav agency, Tangung, regrouped over sixty national agencies, compared with twelve at its founding. The volume of information dealt with is today estimated at sixty thousand words a day, compared to three thousand at its founding.

Regional agencies have also been projected or constituted. Thus, for example, ALASEI (Agencia Latinoamericana de Servicios Especiales de Informacion) was announced in December 1980 by UNESCO; its main objective is to distribute news reports, articles, and analyses, but not news on Latin America from Latin America. The project, developed by a team of Latin American experts and UNESCO, is directed by the deputy director general of UNESCO.[25] In its conception this project took note of several of the numerous suggestions made at the above-cited conferences. Its goal is to aid the participation of all sectors engaged in the process of social communication in what the project considers to be the first step towards a new information and communication policy in Latin America. These sectors include regional associations of journalists; regional organizations of the owners of the means of mass communication; regional organizations of communications researchers; users and receivers of information (a category the project considers to have been the widely ignored); and finally, individual states, to whom the project proposed participation through an existing regional organization like the Latin American Economic System (SELA). The information policy followed insists on the need to valorize structural aspects over conjunctural aspects; the essential over the banal, provisional or transitory; to emphasise dynamic social processes over a static treatment of isolated and contingent facts, to establish a relation of social dynamics between the national and the regional, and to evaluate the situation or the immediate news through common regional objectives. Three themes should run through the information emitted and these are objectives in themselves: the themes of *development, integration,* and *cultural identity.* On the question of development, there is a refusal to conceptualize development as an increase in production or in the productivity of goods and services, in favour of a notion of integral development and integration. Development is integral to the extent that it goes beyond the sphere of the economic activity of Latin American countries and extends to an overall transformation of perceptions, perspectives, and activities that consider the satisfaction of cultural and intellectual needs as much as primary or material needs and that confide in the unlimited capacities of the people to go beyond the current economic and social situation and transform it in the search for a better quality of life. Integration is envisaged to the extent that it is an instrument for the cohesion of societies which, like Latin Americans themselves, have a past and a destiny in common. Cultural identity "is a question of reaffirming the particularity of Latin American culture as the cradle of a diverse plurality, endogenous manifestations that have their point of departure in the heterogeneity of the continent's peoples. Latin America must not be seen as a prolongation of Europe or an appendix of the West but as *another reality* that throws up at each instant surprising illustrations of an irreducible originality. This includes the pre-Colombian heritage, the colonial period, the transformations produced by the continental movement of emancipation, and the survival of a common patrimony that is rigidly opposed to the homogeneity coming from industrialized countries through various forms of so-called culture for the masses."[26] Generally, through the themes preferred and the activities undertaken, it is above all a search for "endogenous potentialities likely to activate an autonomous and self-reliant development" that make self-reliance and self-sufficiency the key to regional integration. This does not mean isolation on a national, regional, or international level, but the contrary, "On the national level, self-reliance constitutes the instrument and strategy for conferring a content on political independence and translating the autonomous capability for making decisions which allow a country to establish relations with other countries on a basis of mutual respect and equality."[27] On paper, the project seems perfect, but the sheer diversity of political regimes coexisting in Latin America could seriously hinder its functioning and limit its scope.

Another example is the news agency of the OPEC countries. It began to transmit from Vienna, an average of fifteen hundred words a day to seventy countries in five continents in November 1980. Its goal is not only to transmit information on energy and related events but also to present an objective and coherent image of OPEC policy. At the end of 1980, the committee of experts of PANA (Pan-African News Agency) met in Dakar to study the investment and running costs of an agency aiming at regional integration in Africa.

These demands by nonaligned countries for a NIIO have not always been well received by countries sheltering the large international news agencies. Karl Nordenstreng distinguishes three main stages: (1) the beginning of a large-scale offensive by developing countries in 1972, supported by the socialist bloc. (2) a counteroffensive by large Western countries and particularly by the main international press agencies (1976–77). (3) consolidation of positions and attempts at reconciliation by Western countries, particularly the United States, which proposed a broad aid program for the development of a communication infrastructure in Third World countries, hoping to thus create new markets for new communications technologies (1977–79).[28] Finally, we could add the current phase that has seen the failure of what had been dubbed the "Marshall Plan of Communications." The arrival of Reagan has drawn together the defenders of the free flow of information under the banner of neo-liberalism: the contradictions have also deepened within the southern countries. The consensus achieved by a certain Third Worldism is crumbling away as economic and political differences bore into the nonaligned countries. Day after day, these contradictions reverberate within the international bodies that have served as a platform and a battleground for a NIIO. Despite their limitations, the importance that these processes have had in forming a consciousness on the world imbalance in information cannot be stressed too often.

In tandem with their demands in front of international organizations like UNESCO or the UN, nonaligned countries have also confronted industrialized countries inside the International Telecommunications Union during the World Administrative Radio Conference (WARC) held in Geneva in 1980 and have contested their monopoly of the radio spectrum. For the first time, organisations, which until then had a strictly technical reputation, began to experience the fallout of an interrogation of the distribution of power of world communications. As a correspondent of *Business Week* wrote in the May 21, 1979 issue, several months before this conference on the distribution of frequencies:

> This year's meeting will be a far cry from the quiet, non-political conferences of the past, when a handful of communications engineers agreed among themselves, and when countries respected ITU decisions even when they were at war with one another. This time, a horde of Third-World nations are determined to use the ITU meeting to further a drive toward

what they call a "new world information order," reflecting their intense desire to have more of a say in the flow of information across their borders. Some key issues are likely to come to a boil. In late April, representatives of these less developed countries (LDCs) were plotting their strategies in closed sessions in Lomé, capital of . . . Togo. That could spell trouble for various segments of U.S. industry, which usually has been able to lock up the frequencies it needed to support new products and markets.

In the course of these debates, some countries like Colombia have proposed new notions like "self-determination of national space." Developed countries have wanted to clear the tropical wave band to use it for international radio broadcasting services, whereas countries like Brazil and India have demanded its maintenance because these waves are of incalculable value for sprawling countries, permitting excellent service at low cost. In the case of Brazil, there are fifty thousand stations operating in this band, which serves as a means of communication for transport firms, agricultural exploitation, and isolated places in the interior.[29] To regulate these differences, WARC agreed that a conference be held in 1983 in order to discuss planning proposals for this spectrum made by nonaligned countries.

National Communication Policies

The second type of activity undertaken by the nonaligned countries refers back in particular to the impetus of national communication policies defined by UNESCO in 1974 as "an integrated, explicit and enduring set of principles and standards of behavior applicable to institutions centrally involved in the mass communication process of a country." Several conferences have been given the task of specifying in more detail the content of this communication policy. Among them, the intergovernmental conference on communication policies in Latin America and the Caribbean, held in San José, Costa Rica, in July 1976 and the intergovernmental conference on the same subject for Asia and Oceania, held in Kuala Lumpur in February 1979.[30] The Costa Rica conference defined communication policy as follows: "Communication policies constitute coherent sets of principles and norms designed to act as general guidelines for communication organs and institutions in individual countries. They provide a frame of reference for the elaboration of national strategies with a view to the setting up of communication infrastructures that will have a function to fullfil in their educational, social, cultural, and economic development. Even when they are not explicitly formulated, there already exist in many countries national communication policies that represent the end result of a process of cooperation and compromise between various partners, namely the public authorities, the media, the professional organizations, and the public, which is the ultimate user."

The Costa Rica conference proposed an enlarging of the intellectual and judicial content of the concept of freedom of expression in order to be able to integrate the problems posed by the access and participation of the people in communication processes. It posed the principles of what it called "the right to communication" in its dual aspect: access and participation. "At the level of infrastructures of access, because of serious gaps concerning the scale of the national territory to be serviced, the transmission of signals and messages on a national and regional scale, and the integration of systems and sub-systems there remain both internal to most countries of the region and between them, unacceptable differences of access to medias and messages." Another essential point: the insistence on the need to assure the access and participation of local communities and the association of emitters and receivers in feedback systems is also a demystification of the media system and an experimentation with alternative means of communication, both of which were advised and promoted by the conference.

If the majority of conferences reuniting nonaligned countries around the theme of information have provoked acrimonious comments from large press agencies and transnational publications, the Costa Rica conference was undoubtedly the one which received the most shrapnel from these same publications, especially the Hearst group. William Randolph Hearst, Jr., wrote, "The threat weighing on the free press today is virtually world-wide, through a vast international conspiracy directed by UNESCO. The latter is one of the anti-democratic agencies commanded by Moscow, which operates in Paris under the flag of the United Nations." At the Costa Rica conference, the participants had noted that "the structures of ownership of the means of communication pose a problem, and they will have to be changed so that they can correspond to the interests, needs, values, and priorities of diverse social sectors, without any discrimination." The Kuala Lumpur conference took note of the recommendations of the preceding one and insisted on the necessity of linking traditional medias and technology transfers by developing endogenous capacities of production and broadcasting/distribution. Another point with a large consensus was the idea of the necessity of codes of conduct or codes of ethics defining the responsibilities of the media in respect to society, on a national and international level.

The balance sheet that can be drawn up regarding the establishment of national communication policies is much more limited than that in the domain of the creation of regional press agencies. This can be explained by the essential fact that the contradictions of Third World ideology that allows countries with sometimes diametrically opposed political regimes to constitute a relatively united front for demand of a NIIO, explode in broad daylight when it is a question of envisaging at the national level the structural implications of a certain conception of communication in which all social sectors participate. Many researchers, mainly Latin American, have emphasized the fact that selecting the subject-state as the unit of this policy relegates the problem of various secondary communities to a secondary level. The Venezuelan, Osvaldo Capriles, has noted the consequences of this Third Worldism and the statist conception of change of communication systems: "There is an excessive predominance of Third Worldism as an over-justification which frequently does not seem to distinguish between democratic, progressive states and totalitarian, reactionary states. Thus, countries of a feudal political texture, enemies of human rights, appear alongside countries which endeavor to advance the economic, political, and cultural liberation of their people. Many Latin American countries and Third World countries have used the NIIO as a 'flight forward' to abandon the demanding and dangerous terrain of national policies, arguing that the priority lies at the international level. The impassioned defence of a new economic order, a new information order, a new technological order, is often, a convenient mask for maintaining an unchanged internal situation."[31] The balance sheet drawn up by Osvaldo Capriles in September 1980 on the application of the recommendations of the Costa Rica conference scarcely gives occasion for celebrating. Referring to Costa Rica, Peru, and Venezuela in particular, all of which played a dominant role at the conference, he notes a marked withdrawl of positions accepting the need for a regulation of the means of communication in terms of a policy of planning for this sector. Capriles dwells on the case of Venezuela.

> Venezuela is a paradigmatic case. The Government has abandoned the RATELVE project, produced by the research sector with the participation of the most qualified representatives of the public sector, the army, the Catholic church, the trade unions etc . . . and has even abandoned legislative projects for advertising and cinema, and control of alcohol and tobacco advertising. On the other hand, it has decided to dignify, next year, private radio and to change what had been up till now precarious "permits" for twelve-year concessions. The inter-weaving of political power with economic power, with the aid of the power of private information

and communication, makes itself felt in pre-electoral periods. The government nourishes the private mass-media sector with economic resources, advertising, loans, credit facilities, subsidies etc, as it fears above all offending this sector which it could, however, silence simply by ending such payments. This shows that the autonomy of the state in respect to mass media apparatuses is minimal, and even less than other aspects of its activity. This is due to the importance of this apparatus for the amplified reproduction of a dependent process and the ideological cohesion of the system of domination.[32]

In Mexico, where the state participates in advertising to the tune of 18 percent of the total receipts, the year 1980 closed with a disappointment of the same nature. In an editorial in the newspaper, *El Dia* on December 20, 1980, under the headline, "The Regulation of the Right to Information: Insistence and Necessity," the following balance sheet is given:

During this year, the right to information has been publicly and systematically discussed. . . . Several months have passed since this right has been analyzed and looked at from all possible angles. But the words remain there, words that seek to define a concept. We know that the development of a law requires a lot of work, particularly when it deals with a complex matter. The legislator rightly pretends that the law must be observed in setting aside as much as possible the shadow of the law's unpopularity. But to meditate overly on laws, on their development with a view to promulgating them is not itself a healthy custom in a democracy; the right to information (its structure, judicial nature, political character) is widely known. What we cannot see clearly is the reason for which a law so desired is not promulgated. This leads us to believe that interests at stake, typically those of enterprises, are putting up an obstacle to its promulgation.

In Mexico 1980 was marked by numerous discussions in the Chamber of Representatives on the implications of the right to information.[33] Three types of proposal can be unravelled from these debates: (1) The need to revise and modify laws, regulations, agreements, and decrees concerning information in a spirit of participation and democratization, along the lines proposed by the final report of the UNESCO MacBride Commission. (2) Incorporation of Mexico in the international pact of civil and political rights formulated in New York on December 16, 1966, article 19 of which guarantees the right to communicate. (3) The taking up of a recommendation of the Costa Rica Conference to create a National Council on Communication Policy in which representatives of academic organizations, trade unions, social groups, and parties can participate, with all organizations having a degree of representation.

If the list of countries that have adopted a national communication policy is relatively limited, on the other hand there is a long list of countries that have taken a limited series of measures, in one way or another, to diminish the extent of foreign penetration. Brazil, where a law protecting local cinema already requires that national films be shown on a certain number of days, discussed in July 1980 new broadcasting legislation requiring that a percentage of television programming be devoted to national programs. A series of measures, included in a report recommending the nationalization of the publishing industry, were envisaged: foreign participation was not to exceed 40 percent in each firm and directors were to be both Brazilian born and resident in the country. The proposed legislation carried an exemption for firms installed in Brazil for ten years or more. A new organization called Prodelivro (Program for the Development of the Book), founded in January 1980, was given the responsibility of furthering discussion and approval of this proposed law. Another provision: the law would require Brazilian publishers to issue a book by a national author for every foreign one. Multinationals made it known that they feared the proposed measure "would quickly reduce the quality as well as the number of high-level cultural and scientific titles available to a nation that is badly in need of them."[34] The nationalization project was aimed above all at textbook production, where according to a Brazilian representative, "In the area of university-level books, foreign houses have frozen out Brazilians by holding onto copyrights, luring Brazilian authors with attractive terms, buying into Brazilian companies."[35] In the list of transnational firms affected, we find Encyclopaedia Britannica, Grolier, Richard Abel, Saunders, McGraw-Hill, Wiley, and Harper & Row; Bertelsman and Ernest Klett from Germany; Salvat and Reverté from Spain; Hachette, Larousse, and Masson from France; Elsevier from the Netherlands.

In July 1980 Venezuela also decreed that television channels had to transmit a minimum of 50 percent of nationally produced programs each week, that is, programs whose artistic and technical realization were 75 percent Venezuelan. It also required the minimum transmission of thirty minutes a day from Monday to Friday of children's programs developed nationally and five hours a week of national programs for young people. As for advertising, it arranged that advertising aimed at adults had to be transmitted after 6 P.M., four times an hour, with a maximum of fifteen minutes an hour, and with a duration of no more than five seconds an advertisement. Also, cigarette advertisements had to carry a health warning. Finally, the duration of *telenovelas* was restricted by forbidding them before 10 P.M.[36] This limited regulation is itself subject to the same unknown risks pointed out by Venezuelan sociologists. The resistance to the creation of a National Communication Council and the finalization of a control body for the quotas imposed is only a consequence of the balance of power existing in the country. Some countries, anxious to protect national artists and workers in shows, films, theater, and so forth, have tried to define what is meant by *national work*. Belgium, particularly threatened by the invasion of foreign radio and television, is among them. To fall within the category *national work,* particularly in the domain of musical production, but also in other domains of cultural production, the instrumental interpretation or vocal piece, or the two, must be principally executed by a national artist; or again, the music must have been written by a national composer or the words, by a national lyricist.[37]

Along the same lines, let us point out the cases of countries where, until recently, foreigners could wholly own firms engaged in the communication industry but which now are increasingly taking measures to limit this ownership. The latest case to date is that of Zimbabwe, which in the name of the protection of its cultural identity, has bought up shares from foreign firms to become master of its own press. The policy in Canada, applied to foreign enterprises like *Readers' Digest,* of a nationalization of the majority of the content as well as a nationalization of ownership, comes from the same inspiration.

Self-Reliance and Communication Technologies

The revival undergone by light communication technologies is well known, as is the mythology accompanying them, as much in the central countries as in the periphery. In a critique of the use of light medias in the Third World, Josiane Jouët notes that too often, these projects, which attempt to put the slogan "small is beautiful" onto the agenda, are based on the error of exaggerating their impact. They "attempt to induce an evolution of the attitudes and behavior of the villagers in ignorance of the decisive influence of socio-economic structures and power factors on the adoption of innovations, brought to the fore by numerous authors. . . . Small media, after the fashion of all technology, are not neutral instruments. The new systems of communication that they generate, small scale or even microsystems, are as much as the mass media integrated into the network of economic and commercial domination of neocolonialism. The dependence on hardware and maintenance services doubles with an exogenous cultural penetration inspiring their 'methods of employment.' "[38]

These new light technologies, which seem less linked to the constraints of centralized media apparatuses, have been associated, sometimes a little too quickly, with self-reliance. They are supposed to constitute the technology par excellence for new, democratic communication networks. The history of Mozambique teaches us that things are not so simple. "The important thing to remember is that 'small' can be 'beautiful' and 'big' can be 'magnificent' only under certain conditions."[39] This affirmation applies to the particular as to the general. Soft, decentralized technologies, as Super-8 cameras, video, and so forth, are labelled, do not necessarily create a soft, decentralized communication. What creates a decentralized communication is the network of decentralized social organisations which it fits into.

Mozambique has very few mass communication means available.[40] The press only covers the large urban centers; the radio network will only cover the whole country towards the end of the 1980s, and the cinema industry is only just beginning. The country's advantage and at the same time its disadvantage is not being able to count on an already well-developed national communication system. Thus, it can prepare a system in keeping with the options of socialism and self-reliance it has chosen. The government has decided to introduce television, taking two precautions. First the television apparatus should not become the motor of a system of communication that marginalizes other modes of communication (traditional or modern, theatre, puppets, dances, songs, etc.) and does not systematically reproduce the social dichotomies of communication systems marked by the influence of mass culture (in particular, the famous rural/urban segregation, which fixes urban references as the center of progress). Second, the television apparatus should not become a transmission belt of a whole system of cultural dependence. As the minister of information said in presenting the first phase of experimentation:

> The central objective of the experimental phase is the training of Mozambican personnel, the apprenticeship in television. In Mozambique, we do not have this knowledge. We need to know television techniques, the equipment, costs, organization, management. We know from the experience of other countries that television determines very high indexes of dependence—technological dependence and political dependence. For this reason, our fundamental preoccupation in carrying out this experimental phase is to be able to evaluate to what extent technological and political dependence makes itself felt in a project of this nature. When we refer to political dependence, we basically refer to the situation we see in other

countries where television is to all intents and purposes dependent on the acquisition of external programs. The latter do not express the values, interests, and preoccupations of the country nor the people and often have a function of diseducation and even alienation.[41]

It is in light of these two principles that we must judge the content of the experimental phase that begun in January 1981. Mozambique has profited from the experience of free television in Italy. In agreement with an Italian firm occupied in its own country with the establishment of democratic networks, the Mozambican government has decided to acquire a broadcasting station at low cost with a range of seventy kilometers despite its small size. Its goal is not only to train technicians but also to learn to communicate with the people—in other words, to learn to know the receivers, to observe their reactions and their capacities for producing messages. This experimental phase is taking place in the capital, Maputo, and its outskirts. Its target-receivers are the organized sector of the population. Television receivers have been distributed in the cultural centers in organized districts and villages. The decision to carry out this phase with light technology allows the country to have the elements it needs for evaluation at the end of the phase without being attached to a model imposed by the manufacturer and the institution installing it. As the minister said, "Television is an extremely advanced, complicated technology; and in underdeveloped countries like ours, we must remain for a long time dependent on foreign techniques, and this constitutes a limitation of freedom. A fortiori, if we proceed with very ambitious projects, this dependence will be strong."[42] The education, health, agriculture, and planning sectors are also associated with the experiment.

However, we must look at other communication projects to see how the Mozambican project is integrated in a wider communication policy from which it takes its philosophy. This is the case of projects of installing communications networks in the *aldeais comunais*. These communal villages, first conceived of as regroupings of the rural population and new forms of organisation, are already in themselves new forms of communication and interrelation between the various rural groups. The origin of the people is diverse. One finds returned refugees from neighbouring countries as well as refugees from strategic villages divided by the Portuguese army to cut off the peasantry from the liberation army. Communal villages combine forms of collective ownership and work on cooperatives with family forms of ownership and work. These production units also have a collective administration. In the course of a mission to Mozambique in October 1980,

Michèle Mattelart, Boubakar Sock, and I carried out an evaluation report for UNICEF and the Mozambican government. The experimental project of social communication unfolding in several communal villages has two fundamental objectives: to put forward information as a factor in the internal development of each one of these villages and service as a laboratory of audiovisual experimentation to guide the setting up of a national communication network and to avert damage inside communes from technological aggression. This project thus presupposes a profound questioning of the vertical character of the established models of communication and aims to substitute a communication made in the name of the people, by the people; more precisely, to gather in concrete problems and local needs for programs and have them expressed by those concerned in order to stimulate collective reflection and resolution of these problems by rank-and-file organizations.

The laboratory is aiming for a dual pedagogy:

First, a *pedagogy of work with different institutions* based on the needs of each community and not from structures based on assistance. The colonial state apparatus was a cumbersome heritage, marked by the compartmentalization of tasks, "departmentalism," which blocked the coordination of various institutions—health, education, agriculture, transport, and so forth. There are also different degrees of sensitivity on the part of the different ministries faced with the need to include an information strategy in their approach strategy to the community. From this point of view, the population can no longer be considered as the receiver of a policy of communication, health, and education but rather as a party in the formulation of the content of this policy. This project could stimulate research on the part of institutions (based on the concrete needs of the population) into methods of approach, language, and a mode of communication with the community. This is not an easy thing to do. This search for an articulation between the base and the ministerial superstructure, conforming to the notion of a real popular participation, will not proceed without conflict, divergences, and a certain lack of synchrony.

Second, the experiment is aiming at a pedagogy of technological introduction because the successful use of new media technology presupposes literacy of electronic images and sound. This pedagogy concerns primarily the appropriation by the people of its local language and the Portuguese language. It presupposes a constant work of research, codification, and systematization of the information gathered. There is a difficulty, for example, in translating into local languages notions belonging to new forms of organization and new references.

Image literacy seeks to produce audiovisual material with a goal of teaching the population the language of the image. It goes without saying that this teaching can only be accompanied by research that takes account of the reactions of the community and its modes of reception and that records and theorizes about them to help them serve as instruments for other experiments in other communities.

All of this presupposes, of course, that traditional forms of communication (songs, dances, oral forms) and written, artisanal forms like wall newspapers, encouraged since 1975, will not be devalued.

This pedagogical approach depends on one precondition—the community's knowledge. This knowledge constitutes the primary work of the animators of these communication cells and is a longer and more important work than is generally thought. The community's knowledge constitutes the first step towards a popular appropriation of reality and the primary content of the messages it will send out.[43]

It is in this same perspective of self-reliance that the Mozambican government, in connection with UNESCO, has decided to create a school of journalism. Given the lack of trained personnel, it proposes to train journalists and communicators at an intermediate level. Let us recall that before Mozambique, Tanzania carried out between 1971 and 1973, numerous video experiments in three Ujamaa villages also in a framework of self-reliance. Other projects were based on photo and cinema.

Self Development and Data Processing Industry

With Brazil, we pass to another technological age and political regime. In the name of national security, but equally of cultural identity, Brazil has attempted since 1972 a self-development of its computer and information treatment industries. Whereas neighbours like Argentina and Chile have renounced the establishment of a national computer and electronics industry (Argentina has only raised the question of national security and of a nuclear energy industry), being content to buy technology from abroad, Brazil has militated for national independence in this domain. The declarations of the Brazilian engineer quoted in Chapter 3 are not chance remarks. The Intergovernmental Bureau for Informatics (IBI) is also a choice tribune to discuss the stakes of new communication systems. Although the IBI is open to all UN members or UN sponsored groups, it is comprised mainly of developing nations.[44]

Let us trace the principal points and phases through which the Brazilian computerization policy has passed. In 1972 an organization for the coordination of data treatment activities was created (CAPRE). This organization was to rationalize the purchase of computer equipment for the federal public administration. Nevertheless, economic problems and the serious balance of payments situation led the government to use CAPRE to control all imports in this domain and to develop national computer enterprises. In 1974, the government decided to reserve the manufacture of mini- or microcomputers for the national market. Reservation for the national market did not signify only a ban on imports but also signified the production of equipment by firms with a majority of national capital. As a Latin American sociologist notes: "Although this technological policy has serious limitations, it is, however, practically unique among Third World countries and is undoubtedly an important step towards the development of our own capabilities in these strategic sectors."[45] In 1974 the decision to create a Brazilian minicomputer industry was taken (Digibras-Empresa Digital Brasileira). In 1977 to strengthen the local computer sector, the government launched a public offer for the local manufacture of minicomputers. American giants like Burroughs presented themselves, but to their frustration, the Japanese firm, Fujitsu; the French information processing firm, Logabax; and the German firm, Nixdorf, were retained. In October 1979 the special Secretariat for Computer Science (SEI), directly linked to the right hand of the government, the Council for National Security, was created.

To put the importance of Brazil in the information processing field into perspective, let us recall that Brazil occupies seventh place behind the United States, Japan, West Germany, Britain, France, and Italy. The SEI has the responsibility for orienting, planning, supervising, watching over, and managing the resources and funds destined for imports, investment, research, service benefits, training of manpower, participation of foreign enterprises, and the restriction of the number of manufacturers for each piece of equipment. The creation of the SEI indicated how much the Brazilian government had become aware of the importance of computer technology and the multiple range of applications. Although in the beginning the SEI was only linked to technical, scientific, and employer sectors of the national community, the SEI attempted a dialogue with more sectors that it had beforehand, motivated by the avalanche of criticism and opposition unleashed in most national sectors by its nuclear energy program. A series of normative acts were taken, for example, provision for the recording at the SEI of all manufacturers of electronic equipment, directly or indirectly linked to information treatment (from calculators to computers); provision for requiring preliminary authorization for the purchase or hiring of equipment by the federal public administration; provision to be given for the purchase of national products by the administration. The idea was also to be able to predict the future needs of the Brazilian government, the biggest purchaser of computer equipment. The balance sheet of this moderately nationalist policy has already given several results. Even if numerous criticisms have come from various technical circles on the defaults of an uncompetitive strategy (too much importance given to central memory banks and units and not enough to key sectors like software and related hardware), the results, judged by the Brazilians' aims, are eloquent. The policy of national reservation for nationally manufactured minicomputers has, however, been violated. On July 6, 1980, IBM and Hewlett-Packard obtained authorization, to the great displeasure of national manufacturers and the scientific community, to produce medium-sized and microcomputers in Brazil. This dispensation has been variously interpreted. The most satisfying interpretation is supplied by Judith Sutz, who situates the conflict of interests opposing various projects when it was a question of defining a self-reliant policy for computerization:

> This first step, won by IBM and Hewlett-Packard, thanks undoubtedly to the July 1980 decree, has consequences for the young Brazilian digital industry that go beyond the production of equipment in itself. For example, these transnationals will have to import basic supplies—integrated circuits, microprocessors, and so forth—which will accelerate the country's minor obsolescence problem and render expansion difficult. This in turn will have consequences for the competitivity of national equipment. Although it seems unreasonable to draw general conclusions from this particular point, it must be wondered to what extent the Brazilian regime is able to lead a nationalist policy in the technological domain if its adversaries are multinationals and large sectors of the bourgeoisie who are allied to them. This conflict reflects a struggle occupying a central role in the problem of technological autonomy: the definition of needs and the national effort to meet them or a technological laissez-faire that always primarily profits foreign corporations.[46]

Presently the transborder data flow and the question of its control are priority subjects for the formulation of a national computer policy. The SEI is encouraging the implantation of local data banks and the maintenance in the country of copies of foreign data banks in case of interruptions to the data flow. At the international level, Brazil is in a ringside seat when it comes to demanding international legislation protecting people against incorrect use of information belonging to them. This demand for technological independence for computers and telecommunications disappears, however, as soon as the question of installation arises. For example, the first experiment in the use of the videotext in Saõ Paulo, based on the French system, Teletel, was scarcely more innovative in its uses than the Giscardian videotext experience. (Note that Brazil, beginning in 1982, is the seventh country in the world to launch this type of electronic service.)

We must look to Canada for the first attempt to impose an overall communication policy that integrates the notion of information in all its aspects. As Oswald H. Ganley noted in *Datamation* (September 1980): "Canada is probably exceptional in the world community in being the first country to recognise the full range of connections among the various communications and information resources across a spectrum which runs from the print media to films and advertising, to broadcasting, to computers, to computer communications, to the telephone and telecommunications systems, to communications satellites, to remote sensing, and to portions of industrial know-how and research and development. Canada has been the first to see and to extensively study the importance of these phenomena to its political processes, its economic policies, and its cultural and legal thinking."[47]

Sweden has proposed the promulgation of a "vulnerability act" in a controversial report entitled *The Vulnerability of the Computerized Society* ("all computer systems are vulnerable to acts of war, terrorism, economic embargo, malnutrition and unintentional errors which can lead to a system breakdown"),[48] and is following the same path as Canada. Already, transnationals are worried.

> The fear in some quarters is that vulnerability will become another issue like transborder data flow which could clip the wings of U.S. multinationals—both vendors and users. By tightening up security requirements on foreign hardware, software and service sources, by insisting on local expertise for systems, by limiting the amount of foreign processing a multinational may do, and by limiting system complexity, a new Swedish Vulnerability Act could set a pace popular with some politicians and others anxious to limit d-p activity as a possible social danger.
>
> Measures proposed by the Swedish report include licensing for public sector computer systems as well as some private sector operations. For businesses designated "K-enterprises" (included on the National Board of Economic Defense List), a system of notification and advice should be established. The report notes that such special business sectors, which include banks, insurance companies, certain parts of the manufacturing

Fig. 1 Marketing Warfare

1. 2,500 Years of War.
In twenty-five minutes, the opening session will summarise twenty-five centuries of military strategy with emphasis on the lessons that marketing people can learn from the victories and defeats on the famous battlefields of the past. Hastings, Agincourt, Quebec, Waterloo, etc.

2. Strategic Planning.
The striking parallels between military planning and marketing planning will be illustrated and discussed. Organisation lines of communication, types of attack, phases of battle.

3. The Strategic Square.
A presentation that introduces concepts of "Offensive," "Defensive," "Flanking" and "Guerrilla Warfare" as applied to marketing.

4. Offensive Warfare.
How to successfully attack the leader to either overtake him or significantly strengthen your position. Emphasis will be placed on the Clausewitz principle of producing a relative superiority at the decisive point by making skillful use of what you have.

5. Offensive Examples.
Case histories illustrating the successful application of offensive warfare will be presented by marketing professionals.

6. Keynote Speaker.
General William C. Westmoreland will offer his personal observations of how an understanding of military principles and strategy can make you a better marketing strategist.

7. Defensive Warfare.
The leader in a category should always protect share. This session will discuss the application of military principles to marketing techniques such as "covering" and "broadening the base."

8. Defensive Examples.
Company case histories.

9. "Fighting Man."
Film clips of the career of U.S. General George S. Patton plus a discussion of personal qualities necessary for leadership of a marketing operation.

10. Flanking Warfare.
An explanation of the classic military principle of avoiding head-to-head confrontations by flanking an opponent.

11. Flanking Examples.
Case histories will illustrate this powerful marketing principle. Special attention will be paid to the importance of new product development in a flanking operation.

12. Guerrilla Warfare.
The special problems and opportunities of the small company. Principles involved are "duration of combat" and "the use of surprise."

13. Guerrilla Examples.
Case histories will demonstrate how small companies can utilise speed and agility to compete in markets dominated by much larger competitors.

14. **Expansion by Diplomacy.**
These presentations will give emphasis to the acquisition process and to the achievement of strategic objectives without open warfare.

15. **Battle for the Mind.**
A presentation that shows how positioning can be used to win the battle for the prospect's mind.

16. **Weapons of the Future.**
The rapid development of micro-technology is providing an impressive array of computing-based weapon systems for marketing warfare.
Weapons for market surveillance, interpretation of marketing intelligence, and for the simulation of campaigns are available in profusion.
The problem will be to match the weapons to the needs of the organisation, and to train the (troops) in their effective use.

17. **War Game.**
Attendees will divide into competitive teams to apply "Marketing Warfare" principles to a real-life marketing dilemma of a key company in the computer. Each team will present its strategy for review by our expert faculty.

What you will learn at the seminar.

1. The four types of marketing warfare and the characteristics of each.

2. How to determine the type of warfare to wage.

3. How to evaluate a situation in terms of offensive, defensive possibilities.

4. How to gather intelligence data before planning an attack.

5. How to use military organisation and thinking in drawing up a strategic plan.

6. How an inferior company can produce relative superiority at the decisive point.

7. How to keep forces concentrated in an overpowering mass.

8. The dangers of line extension. "A Bridge Too Far," in military parlance.

9. How and when to play defence.

10. How to block competitive moves.

11. When and how to launch flanking attacks.

12. The importance of "surprise" and the potential danger of extensive test marketing.

13. The "pursuit" concept and how to exploit it.

14. The principles of guerrilla warfare and the dangers of emulating the leader.

15. The human side of marketing warfare. Why "boldness becomes rarer the higher the rank."

industry, communications and transport concerns, and distributive trades, are considered crucial to the functioning of the country in wartime.[49]

Sweden has indicated that the question of privacy and individual freedom in the face of information, dominant ten years ago, has since slid towards the question of vulnerability, in other words, the question of national security. This is to say that there are numerous ways of being concerned with self-reliance in the domain of new systems of communication.

No one can deny that military vocabulary has now become normal in the discourses both of transnationals and those who oppose them with strategies of regulation. To generic terms like commercial war, economic war, information battle, more specific terms like *food security,* and *information security* have been added; and increasingly the term *national security* borders on that of *cultural identity.* Asked by a journalist of the Caracas daily, *El Nacional* (December 9, 1980) if he considered that the excessive importation of cultural products affected the notion of national security, a Venezuelan general replied: "All these cultural importations undoubtedly deform Venezuelan culture. This dependence must diminish to the extent that we produce our own programs because the basic reason for the importation of this foreign culture is often that a culture void exists that is not filled by our own values. We must develop our expressions. It is only to the extent that we develop a better theater and a better cinema industry that foreign cultural products will be displaced. . . . In any case, when we analyze the pyschosocial aspects influencing security, we include culture."

Military language is equally in fashion among transnationals. This can be illustrated by the content of the seminar held in London by Advanced Management Research International (AMR) in association with the Marketing Society on the theme *marketing warfare* on March 26 and 27, 1979, with the slogan, "What works best in warfare . . . works best in marketing." Among those attending the conference was General Westmoreland, who was invited to discuss the application of military principles in today's marketing arena. The scope and the objectives of the seminar speak for themselves (see Figure 1).

For years, marketing has borrowed from the language of war. Today, companies "launch campaigns," hire "troops" and gather "intelligence." The theory and principles of warfare have developed over the past 2000 years. But marketing, as a discipline, is less than 50 years old. Marketing is long on "'seat of the pants" thinking and short on concepts. Military principles can bridge the gap. The conference has been proven and tested.

It is a unique seminar experience heralded as a classic in the United States. Perhaps the best book on marketing ever published is "On War." Written by a Prussian general, Karl von Clausewitz, the 1832 book outlines the strategic principles behind all successful wars. Now, AMR International in conjunction with the Marketing Society has adapted the axioms of Clausewitz to marketing problems in a two-day seminar called "Marketing Warfare." The seminar will help you increase your strategic skills, whatever the size of your company or the type of your marketplace.

This recourse to military rationality and language in a period of crisis, scarcely hides the confrontation between North and South on the occasion of fixing new rules for the new international division of labor. More and more the demarcation line of the "information industry" in the organization of the world economy is becoming a question that Western countries are establishing as a question of military strategy and Western security.

5

Prospects

Self-Reliance and Democracy

All forms of self-development are not necessarily forms of self-reliance. It is important to remember this elementary observation because this notion is often wrongly applied. If we want to make it a political principle destined to support actions aimed at changing the unequal terms of exchange between the periphery and the centre, we must guard against loose interpretations. The more the notion of self-reliance becomes popular in countries, the more it gathers an international consensus around it, the greater the risk of it losing its revolutionary meaning in relation to development ideologies situated in terms of technocratic modernization and the greater the risk of defusing it politically. We know that concepts and notions represent a terrain of struggle between groups and classes, development projects, and societies. Recent history is full of examples of *semantic expropriations,* confusion being sewn in the conceptual field. The opposition of transnational corporations to a social project in which their activities are regulated, creates almost inevitably a blurring of this conceptual field. However, the nationalism of some peripheral countries wishing to perpetuate acutely unequal structures by invoking national sovereignty, is another powerful factor of diversion of the concept of self-reliance. Stating this is not so much laying down criteria for awarding certificates of self-reliance to those countries fulfilling certain fixed conditions but rather underlining the goal of an approach that takes shelter under the concept of self-reliance. From this point of view, measures aimed at imposing a local content on transnational capital or creating a national, autonomous industrial base are not, strictly speaking, necessarily policies of self-reliance. A national industry can very well satisfy the wants of a middle class elite. At the very most, it can constitute an important step that can be legitimately integrated on the hypothetical day when the majority social forces of a country succeed in making a self-reliant development strategy triumph.

To be able to speak about a self-reliance policy, that is, a policy attempting to subvert the outside development model that corresponds to the logic of expansion of transnational capital, certain fundamental options must be taken that overthrow the established hierarchy of needs that have inspired universal industrialization strategies. A path of self-reliance establishes food, clothing, housing, health, education, self-fulfillment and participation as fundamental needs. Giving priority to these needs comes back to giving priority to certain social actors and it would be difficult to use the expression self-reliance when speaking of the self-development policy of numerous arbitrary states that neither represent their people nor issue from them. As the Venezuelan sociologist quoted in the preceeding section remarked in connection with the NIIO, one should not in the name of a dubious consensus, fall into this quick ratification that places on the same level, under the cover of the genuine demand for an endogenous development, countries with the most disparate political regimes. A fundamental aspect of the philosophy of self-reliance and one of its main contributions is to have posed the question of a democratic development path, that is, a path where participation in the production of society and not only in consumption is recognized as a fundamental need and right of the individual and the group. By setting out its requirements at all levels, individual and collective, local, regional, and national, self-reliance refuses to take the state and its administrative apparatus as the only social subject. It is the multiplicity of organized interlocutors that characterizes a self-reliance situation. A wealth of documentation from popular organizations and movements, consumers' organizations, womens' organizations, environmental movements, human rights organizations, Christian groups, and also the trade-union movement and working-class political parties, shows the extent to which we are witnessing more and more a pressure towards a decentralized development model. As much in the central countries as in the periphery, the emergence of these new historical actors coincides with the profound crisis experienced by historic political movements and parties, which demands a change in the traditional way of conceiving of and making politics. As a Chilean economist has written trying to define the conditions for an effective exercising of national autonomy in the Latin American framework, the renovation of the historical organizations of the popular classes requires "accepting that the structures of the party cannot pretend to control the actions of autonomous social organizations. This means being convinced that trade unions, popular organizations, and professional associations as well as other forms of social mobilization, cannot be considered as the mere appendices of political parties. We must recognize that they have a life of their own and as such represent particular interests. It is from within each people, in each country, in each historical situation that the capacity and decision of popular cohesion must arise as a force for change, from trade unions to womens' groups, from church communities to political parties, from neighborhoods to provinces."[1]

However, let us not fall into naivety. One of the biggest errors that numerous analyses on the strategies of multinational corporations at the moment fall into is only to perceive these principal units of an economic system as bearers of a single project: the centralization, universalization and homogenization of the conditions of their reproduction. This same error thus believes that transnational capital is not the bearer of its own project for decentralization and a decentralized society. This is to misunderstand the powerful restructuring of political, economic, and cultural apparatus that is required so that transnational capital can continue to be deployed. Transnational capital also needs a society splintered into a thousand movements and groups. However, it is only the atomized form of this splintering that is useful to it. In other words, not a chain of movements expressing the solidarity of groups and individuals but a series of monads isolated from one another by competition and individual consumption. The decentralization by the market underlying the transnational project is the bearer of the dismantling of the structures of solidarity. We only have to look at the social uses for the so-called new, participatory technologies proposed by transnational corporations to be convinced of this. This observation situates the challenge posed to the new social movements, which could just as easily serve as embryos of a development project where direct democracy is the order of the day, as reservoirs of relegitimation formulas for the transnational development project. Even if these challenges are much more visible in industrialized countries, it will not be long before peripheral countries crash headlong into them.

The advent of new communications technologies will accelerate the escalation of these challenges. The latest book of Jean-Jacques Servan-Schreiber, *World Challenge,* published simultaneously in thirteen languages, is typical of this mystifying belief in the decentralizing force per se of microelectronic products for the Third World. As Herbert Schiller remarks, "Computer communications, it is evident, are of inestimable value to trans-national corporations and their support structures: the banks, advertising agencies, market research firms, travel companies and the international armed forces of domination. The same cannot be said for the countries in the peripheral world. For weaker nations, the prospect is to be integrated more tightly than ever in unequal relationships. Dependency, rather than being lessened, is likely to be extended. Interdependency, contrary to the assertions of the advocates of transnationalism, is not mutually beneficial to 'host and guest', when power resides, for the most part, with the guest."[2]

We must, therefore, formulate directly the link that must exist between the various struggles and movements of a local and issue-based character and a larger context of struggle where they come to constitute an organic social project. "Local action has a deep political meaning if local self-reliance clearly does not imply any longing for an arcadian archipelago of self-sufficient communities, but rather the promise of a federative society in which free associations would support and strengthen one another. For development, rooted in the primary and local communities, is not only a continuum, but a dialectical process whose local, regional, national, international and global dimensions interact with each other. Just as no local action is historically sustainable outside a truly democratic national structure, there could be no genuine national development that does not support and promote the self-reliance of local communities and derive its relevance and strength from them."[3]

This objective of self-reliance also presents a challenge to the international trade-union movement that they have explicitly taken up. Increasingly, it is accepted that, for a real North-South dialogue to succeed, the different organized social groups that include the union movements of industrialized countries, must be mobilized. Admittedly, this mobilization aiming at the imposition of a new mode of production, consumption, and exchange based on cooperative development, is only beginning. The Federation of Metal Workers (FLM) has clearly indicated the need for such action at the international level. As Alberto Tridente, the secretary of this union, expressed at an international motor workers' conference held in Rome in 1979:

> Without the organized contribution and the coordinated participation of the workers both inside and outside the factories, any attempt at controlling the MNCs would be meaningless and end up fostering a merely formal and mystifying participation while maintaining unchanged the real power

of the management. There is still hard work to be done so that the first painstaking initiatives of international coordination among delegates from the same multinational reach some results in terms of concrete initiatives of struggle.

> In more concrete terms, this means to launch a long and uninterrupted work of organization in the countries where various branches of one same multinational operate. In spite of the differing conditions in which this multinational operates according to the countries, this common factor among workers from various countries will finally allow the launching of a process which, through the establishment of closer international relationships, will lead to concerted actions of workers and labour unions towards the same corporations.[4]

At this conference, the Federation of Metal Workers insisted on the fact that solidarity between European-based unions was no longer sufficient, as many transnationals had their headquarters in the United States or Canada and that even though American unions and workers were often worse than protectionist, "Without their help, we will not be able to combat the transnational corporations." The Federation added: "The American unions themselves are already paying a high price for their national chauvinism. The absence of a class solidarity with Latin America means that USA-based TNCs are able to take advantage of the low wages and shift their investment there. This, again, re-emphasizes the need for organizing direct international solidarity action and fighting to eliminate disparities in wages and conditions in different countries. The FLM managed to organize strikes against the arms trade in support of the struggle in Iran."[5] Concrete questions have been formulated: How are these kinds of direct grass-roots links between workers to be organized? How are they to be supported by research that is detailed and relevant to their needs? How are they to be actively involved in discussing what they discover collectively about the corporations that control, exploit, and divide them? How are their findings and experiences to be shared more widely within the labor movement? And how will the existing international trade union machinery react to these shop floor links?

So many questions, so many lines of action and research. The International Federation of Metal Workers has included among its priorities the struggle against the export to peripheral countries of suspect or polluting industries (runaway hazardous shops) to assure through both laws and collective bargaining that workers are guaranteed the right to refuse hazardous work without reprisal. The question of information networks occupies an essential place. As Barry Castleman points out, after taking stock of the damage from the export of hazardous factories to developing nations, these networks must "disseminate current knowledge about health risks and their controls to industrial workers everywhere, directly and through governments and unions: assist interested governments and affected individuals in appraising industrial project plans and setting standards: gather and distribute knowledge about the movements of hazardous industries around the world: keep track of other aspects of hazard export, primarily the movements of banned foods, drugs, consumer products, and pesticides to other nations from the nation where they were banned."[6] However, as Castleman himself concludes, even if the establishment of international standards and codes is a praiseworthy objective, it is only at the end of the challenging of the need for these discredited technologies and therefore the development models supporting them, that the historical dependence of the periphery on the center will be suppressed.

In recognizing the need to link research and struggles against the negative effects of transnationals, the Federation of Metal Workers also traces a new model of action for social organizations. It also invites us to fill a gap that shows to what extent university research has distanced itself from the preoccupations of the working class and how the trade union movement has not known how to assume its role of *collective intellectual*. The proposal lodged by union organizations for the EEC Commission and the recommendation made by member states to adopt their legislation, that multinationals and large national industrial groups be forced to inform and consult workers on the whole of their activities, are essential links in the creation of this information system. The EEC Commission project that strengthens the consultations already foreseen in the good conduct code adopted by the ILO anticipates forcing headquarters management to send out at least once a week, information on the activities of the whole of its group (economic and financial situation, evolution of production, sales and employment, investment programs, rationalization projects etc.) to its subsidiaries, which in turn, are expected to immediately communicate this information to workers' officials. The transnationals' reaction was not long in coming. Under the title "Labor's Grip on Europe," an editorial in the January 12, 1981 issue of *Business Week* said:

> The purpose of the bill is to strengthen the hand of Europe's trade unions, already strident, aggressive participants in the affairs of companies based in the EEC. The effect would be to freeze the patterns of production and employment by multinationals. Theoretically, the companies would still

have a right to move operations or bring in new methods. But advance notification would give the unions a chance to organize opposition in the communities and in the national legislatures. Europe once was regarded as a highly attractive region for investment. Militant unionism has now given it some of the highest labor costs and strictest work rules in the industrial world. The unions and the political leaders who back them should face the fact that investment does not flow freely into a country when it cannot flow freely out.

On a larger scale, the information exchanges already begun by international consumers' organizations or transnational study groups constitute models to follow. A stocktaking needs to be carried out so that their effects can be developed further. The usefulness of international codes of conducts and consumer protection codes, for example, besides the fact that they allow the identification of problems and the establishment of the normative framework in which local, regional, and national movements can use as their authority, also lies in the fact that their preparation and elaboration are occasions for formal and informal groups to come into contact. We must note that the critique of consumption patterns and through them, models of production and growth, have not up to now been sufficiently considered by the great historical, popular organizations in the periphery as well as the center. Launched in a productivist society, their essentially protest problematic formulation has indirectly created a desire for integration into the various echelons of the so-called consumer society whose principle has only really been called into question by a very small fringe of the workers' movement. The field of cultural consumption is perhaps that which has given rise the least to offensive strategies, as if the domain of the political were limited to the workplace or the repressive state institutions.

It was to run counter to this tendency and to make up for a shortcoming in the workers' movement that a movement attempting to promote what is called in France a *syndicalisme du cadre de vie* (a trade unionism applying to the whole of peoples' lives) has developed in several countries. This involves a unionism of consumers and organizations emphasizing the consumption dimension and its links with everyday reality. We find here the same inspiration as that we mentioned above in connection with the need for an independence and a complementarity between political organizations and diverse social groups and the need to allow free reign to the autonomous expression of social forces that represent the expression of needs unable to be expressed by political groups. These groups are attempting to make up for, in the domain of everyday life, an inadequacy on the part of trade unions whose vocation up to now has been to represent workers in the productive sector.[7]

It is also from within these historic organizations that people in numerous countries have called for the development of reflection and evolution concerning these new problematic formulations more focused on models of everyday life. It would be utopian to think that these new social movements could make a clean sweep of what makes up a patrimony of historical struggle. All realistic strategies that propose to identify the concrete social actors likely to promote activities within a self-reliance framework cannot manage without an appraisal of the way in which existing social organizations have conceived of, materialized, and administered the relation not only between directors and directed, representatives and represented, educators and educated, electors and elected but also the relations between the various components of popular majorities, peasants, workers, lumpen proletariat, ethnic minorities, and between the various components of the family nucleus or the community. Such is the hyperconcrete heritage with which all self-reliance strategies at a local and national level must work.

Central Question of Communication Systems

Through the variety of symptoms touched upon throughout this investigation, we have tried not to lose sight of a central referent: the restructuring of information and communication systems as a political and economic system. On this terrain two radically different projects confront one another. One is inspired by the expansionist logic of transnational capital for which increasingly complex communication networks are necessary to recover from the crisis of productivity and from the crisis of consensus between the various sectors of national communities and the international community. The other is inspired by the desire of peripheral countries committed to the path of self-reliance. They see in the information, culture, and communication between groups, countries, and peoples essential elements for shaking off their dependence on an outside development model. It is the confrontation between these two structural projects that must be taken into account when evaluating but also promoting the limited measures that allow the institution of a new national information order or a NIIO. No particular or limited measure aiming at promoting codes of conduct for advertising or marketing, for example, can be abstracted from this great dynamic.

The field of communications systems is perhaps where the evolution of essential notions like public service and public interest can be most clearly seen. This evolution cannot be understood without questioning the evolution of the nature of the state. Everywhere and more and more the international networks proposed by transnational capital will put pressure on systems run up until now by nation-states. As a study of the Economist Intelligence Unit reported in 1979:

> Private communications systems are undoubtedly a major factor in telecoms demand. Multinational firms are naturally in the van since their intercompany communication needs are obviously great. But equally the use of transmitted data, in banking, distribution, retailing etc is growing enormously. Modern corporations have an increasingly sophisticated approach to this intercommunication—thanks largely to the inefficiencies of PTTs [post, telegraph, and telephone] (particularly international variations in tariffs) and PTT attitude towards new products. Many companies have found it pays to employ a sophisticated telecommunications management system. Unilever is a well-known example in the UK. A company network—Unilever Telecommunications Network (UTN)—is in operation, linking 177 factories and offices. The nodes of this system center on Unilever computers in London, Rotterdam, Leeds and Port Sunlight. The programme optimises costs.[8]

That which applies in the domain of the PTT, where transnational corporations argue the inefficiency of these services in order to surreptitiously introduce their notion of privatization, also applies to the whole field of the advent of new technologies and their relations with various institutional sectors (education, health, etc.), which is the order of the day. The delegation of power by the public sector to the private sector is a fundamental tendency of the transnational capitalist model. Day after day, the economic policies of the large central countries illustrate that they are more and more convinced that the cause of the economic crisis is the growing presence in the economy of the state, which, through its means of assistance-oriented intervention, only fuels the flames of inflation. This indicates that the main problem of the 1980s will be the radical revision of the relations between state and citizen. In the peripheral countries, the extension of the free market economic model—in a context where the mechanisms of civil society are barely expressed, if at all—is also attempting to resolve the crisis of the welfare state. Asking ourselves about the future direction of the state as the expression of determined groups but also the site of social negotiations between the different groups and social classes that make up a nation is therefore a key question for those who seek to further measures of regulation by public authorities. However, to understand this movement of "deconcentration" of some functions of the state, which goes along with a tendency towards the concentration of its repressive functions, two other reflections must be added.

First, the delegation of power by the state, or rather the transfer of competence from the public sector to the private sector, goes hand in hand with the transfer of certain notions legitimizing this public function. Thus, no one can deny that the notion of social responsibility (in the sense where large industrial firms would be capable of self-regulation of their behaviour in respect to their social and economic environment) is one effect of the introduction of the notion of public interest or public service in the field of the private sector.

It is in the light of a double movement that this transformation must be understood. The private sector has to take its inspiration from the goals of the public sector, the probable consequence being the reinforcement of commercial norms and industrial profitability in all sectors of society. The discussions that have arisen over the NIIO have unfortunately been too impassioned to bring out this key element. Large Western countries have been assiduous in accusing Third World countries, wishing to establish the principle of a national information policy, of wanting to impose a totalitarian statist conception of the management of the freedom of expression. On the other hand, Third World countries, confined within an overly large consensus that brings together both democratic and authoritarian regimes, have scarcely had the possibility of directing this discussion into the field of a questioning of the nature of the state and its evolution. This discussion is more and more important and research in this domain must be encouraged; otherwise there is no escape from the idea that self-regulation by transnational corporations is the only way of eradicating their negative effects.

Second, the deconcentration of the function of the state does not only entail advantages for the private sector. If it is certain that its direct result is the commercialization of areas of society that were not so beforehand, it also leads to the widening of the field of intervention for new social organizations that take responsibility for their own interests, no longer being content to delegate them to the guaranteed administrative structures of the public service. However, to clearly understand the impact of this opening, its limits, potentialities, and contradictory challenges, the elements of reflection given at the beginning of this conclusion must be taken up again. The new state will either facilitate the development of transnational firms that will, in any case, have become sufficiently grown up to regulate themselves; or through the deconcentration of its public functions, allow a real decentralization of power in favor of local communities. Decentralized democratic power is becoming an important partner in the determination of models of growth, consumption, and production.

One last observation on the importance of not abstracting from the dynamic underlying the confrontation over the creation of new national or international information order: there is a need to increasingly link not only discussions but also critical research on the NIEO and the NIIO. Many have rightly emphasized that the discussions on the NIIO have been overly marked up till now by the primacy of news reporting. One gets the same impression when consulting the numerous reports on transborder flows of computerized data. The discussions and most of the research on this subject, apart from several rare exceptions, do not go beyond their own sector-based domain. We have said time and time again that it is impossible to understand such and such a sector without linking it to others and without incorporating it into an analysis where the "information industry," in the widest sense, is envisaged as one of the axes of the restructuring of capitalist societies. It is here that gaps in research urgently need to be filled in. *It is also urgent to study the various facets of the transfer of communications technologies to Third World countries (cable television, tele-education, satellites, microprocessors, etc.). Also urgent is the study of the modalities according to which the social implantation of these new technologies are organized as matrices of a restructured society, and the study of how these new technologies are substituted for, or subordinated to, previous communication technologies.* This would be a good occasion to unshackle discussions that have so far occurred in a compartmentalized fashion.

Notes

Chapter 1 / Memorandum for an Analysis of the Cultural Impact of Transnational Firms

1. See A. Mattelart, *Géopolitique du contrôle des naissances* (Paris: Editions universitaires, 1967); B. Mass, *Population Target: The Political Economy of Population Control in Latin America* (Toronto, Latin American Working Group (LARU), 1976); N.J. Demerath, *Birth Control and Foreign Policy: The Alternatives to Family Planning* (New York, Harper & Row, 1976).

2. J.M. Stycos, "Survey Research and Population Control in Latin America," *Public Opinion Quarterly* 28 (Fall 1964).

3. D. Bogue, "Recomendaciones sobre el uso de la comunicación en la educación y motivación para la planificación familiar," in *Boletin del segundo seminario sobre demografía* (Medellín, Colombia: Oct. 1965).

4. D. Bogue, "Some Tentative Recommendations for a 'Sociologically Correct' Family Planning Communication and Motivation Program in India" in C. Kiser, ed., *Research in Family Planning* (Princeton: Princeton University Press, 1962).

5. For more information, see the dossier published by the magazine *Comunicación y cultura* (Buenos Aires and Mexico) 1975, no. 3.

6. L. Garcia dos Santos, *Les déréglements de la rationalité: Etudes sur la démarche systémique du projet SACI/EXERN* (Paris, 1980). Ph.D. thesis directed by A. Mattelart, University of Paris VII).

7. Ibid. Quoted by Garcia dos Santos.

8. On this genealogy see H. Schiller, *Mass Communication and American Empire* (Boston: Beacon, 1971) and A. Mattelart, *Multinational Corporations and the Control of Culture* (Brighton, England: Harvester Press; Atlantic Highlands, N.J.: Humanities Press, 1979).

9. See A. Mattelart and H. Schmucler, *América latina en la encrucijada telemática* (Mexico: Folio, 1983). (English translation, forthcoming).

10. R. Lubar, "Reaganizing the Third World," *Fortune,* November 16, 1981.

11. T. Adorno and M. Horkheimer, "The Culture Industry," in J. Curran et al., eds., *Mass Communication and Society* (London: Edward Arnold, 1977).

12. F. Machlup, *The Production and Distribution of Knowledge in the United States* (Princeton: Princeton University Press, 1966).

13. M.U. Porat, "Emergence of an Information Economy," *Economic Impact,* 1978 no. 4.

14. Z. Brzezinski, *Between Two Ages: America's Role in the Technetronic Era* (New York: Viking Press, 1970).

15. See N. Garnham, "Contribution to a Political Economy of Mass Communication," *Media, Culture and Society* 1, no. 2, (April 1979); A. Mattelart and J.M. Piemme, *Télévision: enjeux sans frontières. Industries culturelles et politique de la communication,* (Presses Universitaires de Grenoble, 1980).

16. UNESCO, *Cultural Industries. A Challenge for the Future of Culture* (Paris: UNESCO Publication, 1982).

17. K. Sauvant, "Multinational Enterprises and the Transmission of Culture: The International Supply of Advertising Services and Business Education," *Journal of Peace Research* 13 no. 1 (1976).

18. M. Crozier, S. Huntington, J. Watanuki, *The Crisis of Democracy: Report on the Governability of Democracies to the Trilateral Commission* (N.Y.: New York University Press, 1975).

19. Ibid.

20. On the transnationalization of the Chilean economy see I. Letelier and M. Moffitt, *Human rights, Economic Aid and Private Banks: The Case of Chile* (Washington: Institute for Policy Studies, 1978).

21. G. Arroyo, "A propos de la dépendance," *Amérique latine,* Paris, Oct–Dec. 1980.

22. *Ibid.*

23. On the history of communication-critical research, see A. Mattelart and S. Siegelaub, eds., *Communication and Class Struggle* (New York: International General Editions, vol. 1, 1979; vol. 2, 1982).

24. E. Fuenzalida, "Incorporation into the Contemporary Stage of the Modern World System: Conditions, Process and Mechanisms," Stanford University, April 1980, Paper.

25. K. Sauvant, "The Poor Countries and the Rich—a Few Steps Forward," *Dissent,* Winter 1978.

26. G. Corm, "Au rebours du développement," *Le monde diplomatique,* Nov. 1980.

27. "The Arusha Declaration (1967)," reprinted in J. Galtung, P. O'Brien, R. Preiswerk, eds., *Self-Reliance: A Strategy for Development,* (London: Bogle–L'Ouverture Publications, 1980).

28. See for instance Galtung et al., Ibid.

29. "The Cocoyoc Declaration (1974)," reprinted in Galtung et al. (ibid).

30. S. Machel in *Ciencia e tecnologia* 1, no. 1 (August 1980).

31. "Global Development: The End of Cultural Diversity. An Ifias Statement," reprinted in Galtung et al., *Self-Reliance* (n. 27).

Chapter 2 / Principal Features of the Cultural Networks

1. M. Mattelart, "Network," *Encyclopaedia Universalis* (Paris, 1978).

2. OECD (Organisation for Economic Co-operation and Development), *Recent Trends in International Direct Investment,* Committee on International Investment and Multinational Entreprises, 1980, draft.

3. *Le Monde,* Paris, February 3, 1981.

4. OECD, *Recent Trends.*

5. "The U.S. Lead in Service Exports is Under Siege," *Business Week,* Sept. 15, 1980.

6. See Mattelart, *Multinational Corporations and the Control of Culture.*

7. "CBS: When Being No. 1 Isn't Enough," *Business Week,* May 26, 1980.

8. Ibid.

9. "Editorial," *Advertising Age,* January 15, 1979. For more information about concentration of ownership in the U.S. mass communications industry, see B.M. Compaine, ed., *Who Owns the Media?* New York: Harmony Books, 1979).

10. A. and M. Mattelart, *De l'usage des médias en temps de crise* (Paris: Alain Moreau, 1979).

11. V. Coppola et al. "Now, Its Superhype," *Newsweek,* Oct. 23, 1978.

12. "Coke's High-Priced Bid for Entertainment," *Business Week,* Feb. 1, 1982.

13. P.J. Schuyten, "How MCA Rediscovered Movieland's Golden Lode," *Fortune,* November 1976.

14. See Schiller, *Mass Communication and American Empire.*

15. "Exxon's Next Prey: I.B.M. and Xerox," *Business Week,* April 28, 1980.

16. "I.B.M.'s Video Play for Consumer Dollars," *Business Week,* Sept. 17, 1979.

17. "A Comedy of Errors Ends a Videodisc Venture," *Business Week,* March 1, 1982.

18. On the Matra-Hachette Merger, see *Le Monde,* Paris, Dec. 11 and 17, 1980.

19. "The Groups: A Time for Consolidation," *Publishers Weekly,* Oct. 1980; "The Realm of Reinhard Mohn," *Business Week,* June 9, 1980.

20. G. Murdock and P. Golding, "Beyond Monopoly: Mass Communications in an Age of Conglomerates," in P. Beharrel and G. Philo, eds. *Trade Unions and the Medias* (Macmillan, 1977).

21. "Britain: U.S. Publishers Invade in a Troubled Book Market," *Business Week,* Dec. 15, 1980. To all these considerations, the dominance of American advertising and marketing firms must be added. The advertising industry undoubt-

edly constitutes the sector of transnational communication where the movement towards concentration is the most pronounced at the moment. To give but one example, in 1978 one of the principal world advertising agencies, Lintas, the majority of whose capital was held by European interests, was bought by the American group, Interpublic, owner of McCann Erickson among others. This group's revenues for 1979 totalled nearly $3 billion, that is, nearly six times as much as the French group, Publicis. However, France is the only European country where the presence of American agencies is a minority one (36 percent of the French market in 1979 compared to 10 percent in 1969) and where the two biggest advertising agencies are of French capital. The situation is completely different in bordering countries. In Italy, Belgium, and Germany, subsidiaries of McCann Erickson, J. Walter Thompson, and Young and Rubicam largely occupy the top positions, whereas in Great Britain the ten biggest agencies are either entirely American or associates of American firms. This hegemony is reproduced at the level of advertisers, which are everywhere transnational firms, invariably the same ones.

22. See A. Mattelart and J.M. Piemme, *Télévision: Enjeux sans frontières,* chapter "Industrie de l'audiovisuel et nouvelle division internationale du travail."

23. In *Libération,* Paris, Sept. 18, 1980.

24. "Los japoneses invaden el mercado de TV con nuevas series de dibujos animados," *Excelsior,* Mexico, Dec. 6, 1980.

25. N. Poulantzas, "L'internationalisation des rapports capitalistes et l'Etat-nation," *Les Temps Modernes,* Feb. 1973; A. Mattelart, *Multinational Corporation and the Control of Culture;* A. and M. Mattelart, *De l'usage des médias en temps de crise,* chapter "La culture intérieure."

26. Y. Agnes, "J.L. Servan Schreiber: la presse à l'américaine," *Le monde du dimanche,* Dec. 23, 1979.

27. P. Besenval, "Images fixes, images mobiles," *Le français d'aujourd'hui,* no. 52, Dec. 1980.

28. P. Flichy, *Les industries de l'imaginaire* (Presses Universitaires de Grenoble, 1980).

29. Ibid.

30. T. Guback, "Film as International Business," *Journal of Communications* 24, no. 1 (Winter 1974).

31. Quoted in T. Guback and T. Varis, *Transnational Film and TV,* report to be published by UNESCO.

32. Report from the Commercial Department, French Embassy, Mexico, CFCE, [Centre Français du Commerce Extérieur], Paris, 1978.

33. L. Liberman et al., *El fenomeno cine: panorama historico de la consolidación de la industria cinematografica nacional* (Mexico, July 1980, unpublished report).

34. S. Sokhona, "Notre cinéma," *Cahiers du Cinema,* Paris, Feb. 1978.

35. B. Boonyadetmala, "Influence of the Transnational Media in Thailand," in Guback and Varis, *Transnational Film and TV* (n. 31).

36. Quoted in Guback and Varis, *Transnational Film and TV.*

37. "Making the Movies into a Business," *Business Week,* June 23, 1973.

38. "An Exclusive Interview with Eric Pleskow, President United Artists," *Cannes Film Daily,* no. 7, May 19, 1977; "An Interview with Myron D. Karlin, President of Warner Brothers International," *Cannes Film Daily,* no. 8, May 20, 1977.

39. J.M. Wilson, "The Global Film: Will it Play in Uruguay?" *New York Times,* Nov. 26, 1978.

40. M. Jokela, "Book, Film, Television—An International Comparison of National Self-Sufficiency in Three Media," (University of Tampere, Finland, 1975, paper. See also the dossier on the Asian cinema published by *Cahiers du Cinema,* Paris, Feb. 1981.

41. J. Forkan, "Middle East Video Recorder Market Built on Piracy," *Advertising Age,* Nov. 12, 1979.

42. Ibid.

43. Ibid.

44. K. Nordenstreng and T. Varis, *Television Traffic—A One-Way Street? A Survey and Analysis of the International Flow of Television Programme Material* (Paris: Unesco, 1974).

45. A. and M. Mattelart, *De l'usage des Médias en Temps de Crise.*

46. Guback and Varis, *Transnational Film and TV.*

47. R. Cruise O'Brien, "Professionalism in Broadcasting: Issues of International Dependence," (discussion paper, Institute of Development Studies, University of Sussex, Dec. 1976).

48. A. Mattelart, *Agresión desde el espacio* (Buenos Aires and Mexico, Siglo XXI, 1972).

49. A. Pasquali, *Para comprender la comunicación,* (Caracas: Monteavila, 1980).

50. M. Soramaki and J. Haarma, *The International Music Industry* (Oy. Yleisradio Ab./Finnish Broadcasting Co., June 1980, paper).

51. "Yes, Nós Temos Cultura," *Veja,* Saõ Paulo, July 20, 1977.

52. *Advertising Age,* April 14, 1980.

53. Center on Transnational Corporations, *Transnational Corporations in Advertising* (New York: United Nations, 1979).

54. "Foreign Ad Agencies Earn their Stripes in '79," *Advertising Age,* April 14, 1980.

55. H. Noorani, "Nigerian Ad Expenditure up 70%," *Advertising Age,* June 11, 1979.

56. D. Chase, "Agencies Set Sight on Latin America, Far East," *Advertising Age,* Sept. 8, 1980; C. Endicott, "Ad Growth Mirrors Rise in World Living Standard," *Advertising Age,* April 30, 1980.

57. A. Santa-Cruz and V. Erazo, *Compropolitan: el orden transnational y su modelo femenino* (Mexico: Ilet/Editorial Nueva Imagen, 1980).

58. Center on Transnational Corporations, *Transnational Corporations in Advertising.*

59. A. Montoya Martin del Campo, *Los determinantes nacionales y transnacionales de la información en Mexico* (Mexico, 1980, unpublished report).

60. C. Endicott, "Ad Growth"

61. J. Honomichl, "Research Top 20 Companies Posted 19% Gain Last Year," *Advertising Age,* April 24, 1978.

62. *Advertising Age,* Sept. 29, 1980.

63. R.A. Amaral Vieira, ed., *Comunicação de massa: o impasse brasileiro* (Rio de Janeiro: Forense Universitaria, 1978).

64. K. Weihe et al., *Publicité et relations publiques des industries d'armement* (Paris: UNESCO, Commission internationale d'étude des problèmes de communication, 1980), doc. no. 50.

65. See Mattelart, *Multinational Corporations and the Control of Culture,* chapter "Upsets in the Cinema and the Press."

66. " 'Rd': The National Book on an International Level," *Advertising Age* (Europe), March 26, 1979.

67. B. Kanner, "U.S. Publishing Moves Abroad Must Shed Made-in-U.S. Image," *Advertising Age,* April 9, 1979.

68. *Ibid.*

69. " 'RD': The National Book on an International Level."

70. B. Kanner, "U.S. Publishing Moves Abroad."

71. See *Hachette la pieuvre: Témoignage d'un militant CFDT* (Paris: Librairie La Commune, 1973).

72. H. Lottman, "Brazil: A Long Way to Go," *Publishers Weekly,* Nov 21, 1980.

73. Mattelart, *Multinational Corporations and the Control of Culture.*

74. P. Golding, "The International Media and the Political Economy of Publishing," *Library Trends,* Spring 1978.

75. Quoted in A. Hasan, *Le livre dans les pays multilingues* (Paris, UNESCO, 1977), Etudes et Documents, no. 82.

76. T. Gil, "La cultura tras los utiles escolares," *Uno más uno,* Mexico, Aug. 15, 1980.

77. F. Reyes Matta, "El encandilamiento informativo de América latina," in F. Reyes Matta, ed., *La información en el nuevo orden internacional* (Mexico: Ilet, 1977).

78. M. Magrebi in *Communication et information,* Québec, vol. III, no. 2 (winter 1980).

79. *El Universal,* Mexico, July 30, 1980.

80. *Advertising Age,* July 16, 1979.

81. *Advertising Age,* March 26, 1973.

82. K. Sauvant, "Multinational Enterprises."

83. "U.S.-Style MBA Programs Catch on in Europe," *Report from Europe, Chemical Bank* 3, No. 4 (May 1976).

84. "Latin Americans Trained in PCC Micro Sales," *Computer World,* January 21, 1980.

85. *Survey of Venezuelan Market for Computers and Related Equipment,* Dec. 1979, unpublished.

86. D. Cudaback, "French Language Law Beginning to Worry Foreign Marketers," *Advertising Age,* March 21, 1977.

87. Quoted by S. Cacaly, "L'information scientifique et technique aux Etats-Unis," *Documentaliste,* Paris, Jan.–Feb. 1977.

88. *Ibid.*

89. A. Iljon, "Bases de données scientifiques et techniques d'une société multilingue," in *CEE, troisième congrès européen sur les systèmes et réseaux de documentation (Luxembourg, 3/6 mai 1977)* (Munich: Verlag Dokumentation, 1977), vol. 1. See also B. Cassen, "La langue anglaise comme véhicule de l'impérialisme culturel," *L'homme et la société,* nos. 47–50, Jan.–Dec. 1978; G. Gablot, "L'anglais, langue scientifique française," *Banque des mots,* Conseil international de la langue française, 1979, no. 16.

90. *Le monde de la médecine,* March 5, 1980.

91. *Publishers Weekly,* April 10, 1978.

92. J. Kirchner, "Se demanda el control nacional de los sistemas de información," *Computerworld/Mexico,* August 25, 1980.

93. *Transnational Corporations in International Tourism* (New York: United Nations, Commission on Transnational Corporations, April 8, 1980).

94. *Service World International (SWI)—Annual '100',* 1978.

95. " 'RD': The National Book on an International Level."

96. S. Downer, "Geografia Universal Sees Growth Ahead," *Advertising Age,* July 16, 1979.

97. Quoted by M. Mattelart, *La cultura de la opresión femenina* (Mexico, Editorial Era, 1977).

98. *Advertising Age,* Jan. 13, 1969.

99. M. Mattelart and M. Piccini, "La televisión y los sectores populares," *Comunicación y cultura,* Buenos Aires and Mexico, no. 2, 1974.

100. Interview with F. Shakespeare, "Who's Winning the Propaganda War," *U.S. News & World Report,* May 1, 1972.

101. *Broadcasting,* Dec. 9, 1974.

102. K. Lynch, "Adplomacy Faux Pas Can Ruin Sales," *Advertising Age,* International Section, Jan. 15, 1979.

103. *Business Week,* April 17, 1978.

104. N. Careem, "Hong-Kong Flocks to Kui Mo Ba Under the Arches," *Advertising Age,* Nov. 21, 1977.

105. Definition by S.B. Rosenblatt *et al.* quoted in J.R. Emmel, "Non-Verbal

Communication as an Intercultural Motivating Factor in Japanese Enterprises"
(Paper, thirtieth annual conference of International Communication Association
(ICA), 1980).

106. J.R. Emmel, ibid.

107. Ibid.

108. M. Pages, M. Bonetti, V. de Gaulejac, D. Descendre, *L'emprise de
l'organisation* (Paris, Presses Universitaires de France, 1979).

109. B. Mennis and K. Sauvant, "Multinational Corporations, Managers, and
the Development of Regional Identifications in Western Europe," *The Annals of the
American Academy of Political and Social Sciences* 403 (Sept. 1972).

110. Quoted by Sauvant, "Multinational Enterprises."

111. "Introduction," *Communication and Class Struggle*, vol. 1.

112. A. Dorfman and A. Mattelart, *How to read Donald Duck* (New York: International General Editions, 1975).

113. J.L. Boutillier, et al., *Le tourisme en Afrique de l'ouest* (Paris, François Mas-
pero, 1978).

114. H.J. Frundt, *Objeciones de accionistas cristianos contra la G. & W., Republica
Dominicana* (Santo Domingo: Publicaciones Estudios Sociales, 1980).

115. E. Fox de Cardona and L.R. Beltran, *La comunicación dominada* (Mexico,
Ilet-Editorial nueva imagen, 1980).

116. Mattelart and Siegelaub, eds., "Introduction," *Communication and Class
Struggle*, vol. 1.

117. R. Berman, "Advertising and Social Change," *Advertising Age*, April 30, 1980.

118. *Advertising Age*, Nov. 21, 1973.

119. Tom Dillon, *Advertising Age*, Nov. 21, 1973; Tom Dillon, *Never Boil an
Alarm Clock* (Batten, Burton, Durstine, and Osborne Agency, 1978).

120. *The New York Times*, Sept. 10, 1977.

121. Letelier and Moffitt, *Human Rights*.

122. R. Bechtos, "Key Consumer Goods Growing Fast in Brazil; Ad Budgets
Keep Pace," *Advertising Age*, March 5, 1973.

123. J.M. Perry, *The New Politics. The Expanding Technology of Political Manip-
ulation* (Weidenfeld & Nicolson, 1968).

124. L.P. Costa and E. Siqueira, "Eis o satelite brasileiro de comunicaçoes,"
Estado de Sao Paulo, April 18, 1976.

125. B. Brecht, *Ecrits sur la littérature et l'art: I. Sur le cinéma* (Paris: L'Arche,
1970).

126. M. Mattelart, "Les Femmes et l'ordre de la crise," *Tel quel*, Paris, no. 74,
winter 1977.

Chapter 3 / The Socio-Cultural Impact of Transnational Firms

1. E. Contreras et al. *L'information audio-visuelle transculturelle*, Etudes et documents, no. 77 (Paris: UNESCO, 1976).

2. *Advertising Age,* May 15, 1978.

3. B. Donath, "JWT in South Africa Reaches out to Blacks," *Advertising Age,* April 25, 1977.

4. See A. Mattelart, "Notes on the Ideology of the Military State," in Mattelart and Siegelaub, eds., *Communication and Class Struggle.*

5. E. Schmidt, *Decoding Corporate Camouflage U.S. Business Support for Apartheid* (Washington: Institute for Policy Studies, 1980).

6. *Profiteering from Cheap Labour Wages Paid by British Firms in South Africa* (London: South Africa Labour Education Program, 1980). See also United Nations Center on Transnational Corporations, *The Activities of Transnational Corporations in the Industrial, Mining and Military Sectors of Southern Africa* (New York, United Nations, 1980).

7. E. Santoro, *La televisión venezolana y la formación de estereotipos en el niño* (Caracas: Universidad Central de Venezuela, 1969).

8. Mattelart and Piccini, "La televisión y los sectores populares."

9. SPP—Secretaria de programación y presupuesto, *Política informática gubernamental* (Mexico, 1980). See also A. Mattelart, H. Schmucler, *América Latina en la encrucijada telemática.*

10. J. Firebrace, *Imported Milk Powders and Bottle Feeding: The Evidence from the Yemen Arab Republic* (Catholic Institute for International Relations, War on Want, 1979).

11. D. Perrot, "Réflexions pour une lecture de la domination à partir des objets," *Encrages,* University of Paris-Vincennes, no. 1 (March 1979).

12. Quoted in *Les sociétés transnationales dans l'industrie alimentaire et les boissons,* report of the Secretariat, Commission on Transnational Corporations (New York, UN, April 17, 1980).

13. A. Chetley, *The Baby Killer Scandal* (London: War on Want, 1979).

14. P. Borgoltz, *Economic and Business Aspects of Infant Formula Promotion: Implications for Nutrition Policy in LDCS—A Report Submitted to UNICEF/WHO,* ITHACA, Cornell University, 1979, unpublished.

15. Ibid.

16. Chetley, *The Baby Killer Scandal.*

17. B. Khindaria, "New Code Could Curb Marketing," *Financial Times,* Dec. 15, 1980.

18. J. Masini et al. *Les multinationales et le développement: trois entreprises et la Côte d'Ivoire* (Paris, Presses Universitaires de France, 1979).

19. Ibid.

20. Ibid.

21. J.E. Austin, "Attacking the Protein Problem" in D. Walcher, N. Kretchmer, and H. Barrett, eds., *Food, Man and Society* (New York and London: Plenum Press, 1976).

22. P. Diener, K. Moore, and R. Mutaw, "Mead, Markets and Mechanical Materialism: The Great Fiasco in Anthropology," *Dialectical Anthropology* 5, no. 3 (Nov. 1980).

23. S. Corro and G. Correa, "Coca-cola: aprovechan el fisco para ampliar sus monopolios," *Proceso,* Mexico, no. 193, July 14, 1980.

24. See United Nations, Commission on Transnational Corporations, *Les sociétés transnationales dans l'industrie alimentaire et des boissons,* New York, April 17, 1980.

25. See the dossier "Transnationales et agriculture en Amérique latine," by G. Arroyo, S. de Almeida, J. Von der Weid, *Amérique latine,* Paris, no. 1, Jan–Feb. 1980.

26. *Excelsior,* Mexico, August 11, 1980.

27. On the fast foods internationalization, see A. and M. Mattelart, *De l'usage des médias en temps de crise,* chapter "Les enfants des Mac (Luhan et Donald)."

28. A. Montoya Martin del Campo, *Los determinantes nacionales y transnacionales.*

29. F. Rello, R. Montes de Oca, and G. Escudero, "La industria agroalimentaria," (Mexico, 1980, unpublished report).

30. J. Chonchol, "Problèmes alimentaires en Amérique latine, malnutrition et dépendance," *Amérique latine,* Paris, no. 4, Oct.–Dec. 1980.

31. Oficina de Asesores del C. Presidente, *Sistema alimentario mexicano: Primer planteamiento de metas de consumo y estrategia de produccion de alimentos basicos para 1980–1982* (Mexico, March 1980).

32. T.F. Ryan, "La pêche en transition à Niué," *Journal de la société des océanistes,* Paris, issue on "Fishing in Oceania" (forthcoming).

33. Center on Transnational Corporations, *Transnational Corporations and the Pharmaceutical Industry* (New York, United Nations, 1979).

34. See the dossier established by *Iztapalapa: Revista de Ciencias Sociales y Humanidades* (Mexico) 1, no. 2 (Jan.–June 1980).

35. *Transnational Corporations and the Pharmaceutical Industry.*

36. V.M. Soria, "Estructura y comportamiento de la industria farmacéutica en Mexico," *Iztapalapa* (Mexico) 1, no. 2, Jan–June 1980.

37. Quoted in C. Medawar, *Insult or Injury: An Enquiry into the Marketing and Advertising of British Food and Drug Products in the Third World* (London: Social Audit, 1979).

38. V.M. Bernal Sahagún, "Las empresas transnacionales y el 'desarrollo' de la industria de la salud en Mexico," *Iztapalapa* 1, no. 2.

39. Quoted in Medawar, *Insult or Injury.*

40. Ibid.

41. Ibid.

42. A. Fazal, "Brave and Angry: The International Consumer Movement's Response to TNCs," *IFDA (International Foundation for Development Alternatives) Dossier* 21 (Nyon, Switzerland, Jan.–Feb. 1981).

43. F. Moore Lappe, "The Population Fix," ibid.

44. The Haslemere Group, *Who Needs the Drug Companies?* (London: War on Want, 1980).

45. Moore Lappe, "The Population Fix."

46. B. Castleman, "The Export of Hazardous Factories to Developing Nations," *International Journal of Health Services* 9, no. 4 (1979).

47. T. Morales Cardona, "El uso de la ciencia y la tecnologia en Puerto Rico con fines coloniales," *Undécima tesis,* Puerto Rico, special edition, vol. 2 nos. 2–3, Oct. 1976.

48. B. Castelman, "The Export of Hazardous Factories."

49. UNESCO, *Les effets du tourisme sur les valeurs socio-culturelles,* (Paris, 1975).

50. H. Give, "De prodigieux atouts touristiques," *Le Monde,* July 18–19, 1976.

51. See E. de Kadt, ed., *Tourism—Passport to development* (Oxford University Press, 1979).

52. J.L. Maurer, *Tourism and Development in a Socio-Cultural Perspective. Indonesia as a Case Study,* (Geneva, Institut Universitaire d'études du développement, Sept. 1980).

53. See J. Bugnicourt, *Le tourisme en Afrique: moteur ou entrave pour le développement?* (Daker: Program "Training for the Environment," 1975).

54. Ibid.

55. E. Ntanyungu and F. N'Duhirahe, *Tourisme et dépendance: la cas de l'Afrique noire* (Geneva: Institut Universitaire d'études du développement, August 1980).

56. H.J. Frundt, *Objeciones de accionistas.*

57. T. Takeo, "Free Trade Zones and Industrialisation of Asia," *Ampo Japan-Asia Quaterly Review,* June 1977.

58. H.J. Frundt, *Objeciones de accionistas.*

59. M. Barang, "La prolifération des zones franches en Asie," *Le Monde diplomatique,* Jan. 1981.

60. R. Trajtenberg, *Transnacionales y fuerza de trabajo en la periferia* (Mexico: Ilet, 1978).

61. Ibid.

62. "U.S. Runaway Shops on the Mexican Border," *Nacla's Latin America and Empire Report* (New York) 9 no. 5 (July–August 1975).

63. A. Sivanandan, "L'impérialisme à l'age du Silicium," *Politique d'aujourd'hui* (Paris), March–April 1980.

64. D. Druijt and M. Vellinga, "Estado, empresa transnacional y movimiento obrero en las economias de enclave: el caso de la Cerro de Pasco corporation en Perú (1902–1974)" in J. Somavia *et al.* eds., *Movimiento Sindical y empresas transnacionales* (Mexico: Ilet-Editorial Njeva Imagen, 1979).

65. A. Mattelart, "Firmes multinationales et syndicats jaunes dans la contre-insurrection," *Les Temps Modernes* (Paris), no. 342, Jan. 1975.

66. *El DIA,* Mexico, July 24, 1980.

67. B. Hamdouch, *Les firmes transnationales et les pays sous-développés: Quelques réflexions suggérées par l'exemple du Maroc* (Rabat: Isea, 1980, paper). See also the research of C. MICHALET and the Centre d'études et de recherches sur l'entreprise multinationale (CEREM), Université de Paris X–Nanterre.

68. See D. Ehrenreich and A. Fuentes "Special report: Life in the Global Assembly Line," *Ms,* January 1981.

69. Quoted by M. Barang, "La prolifération des zones franches en Asie."

70. "U.S. Runaway Shops on the Mexican Border."

71. *Obreras de zona franca: mujeres dominicanas* (Santo Domingo: CEDEE, 1979).

72. "Special Report: Life on the Global Assembly Line."

73. R. Pearson and D. Elson, *Internationalisation of Capital and its Implications for Women in the Third World* (Sussex, England: Institute of Development Studies, 1978); quoted by S.S. Green, *Silicon Valley's Women Workers: A Theoretical Analysis of Sex-Segregation in the Electronics-Industry Labor Market* (Honolulu, Hawaii: East-West Center, 1980).

74. *Obreras de zona franca: mujeres dominicanas.*

75. Ibid.

76. Ehrenreich and Fuentes, "Special report." For more information see *The Changing Role of Southeast Asian Women* (Berkeley: Southeast Asia Resource Center, 1980); L.Y.C. Lim, *Women Workers in Multinational Corporations: The Case of the Electronics Industry in Malaysia and Singapore,* Michigan Occasional Papers in Women's Studies (Ann ARBOR, Mich.: 1980).

77. E. Feder, *El imperialismo fresa* (Mexico: Editorial Campesina, 1977).

78. See M. Mattelart, "Notes on 'Modernity': A Way of Reading Women's Magazine," in *Communication and Class Struggle;* from the same author, *Women and the Cultural Industries,* Cultural Development Series (Paris, UNESCO, 1982).

Chapter 4 / Regulatory Efforts and Policies

1. G. Arroyo, "A propos de la dépendance."

2. G.M. Feldman, "Coping with New Challenges to Investment Venture Abroad," *Commerce America,* July 17, 1978.

3. A. Mattelart, *Mass Media, Ideologies and the Revolutionary Movement* (Brighton, England: Harvester Press; Atlantic Highlands, N.J.: Humanities Press, 1980).

4. "Few Regulators can Out-Peru the Peruvians," *Advertising Age,* International Section, January 15, 1979.

5. Ibid.

6. "Thailand Ad Laws Could Promote Arbitrary Rulings," *Advertising Age,* International Section, June 11, 1979.

7. Comisión preparatoria del Consejo nacional de la cultura, *Proyecto Ratelve (Diseño para una nueva politica de radiodifusión del Estado Venezolano)* (Caracas: Editores Libreria Suma, 1977).

8. Ibid.

9. O. Capriles, *El estado y los medios de comunicación en Venezuela,* (Caracas: Ininco-Universidad Central de Venezuela, 1976).

10. Ministerio de información y turismo, Plan sectorial sobre comunicación social

inserto en el VI plan de desarrollo nacional de la republica (Caracas: Twelfth Assembly and Scientific Conference of the International Association Research [AIERI-IAMCR], August 1980).

11. M. Graziano and E. Safar, *Observaciones en torno a la versión preliminar del plan sectorial sobre comunicación social* (Caracas, Ininco, 1980), paper.

12. P. Borgoltz, *Economic and Business Aspects.*

13. See Chetley, *The Baby Killer Scandal.*

14. P. Borgoltz, *Economic and Business Aspects.*

15. C. Medawar, *Insult or Injury.*

16. Ibid.

17. See for instance, U.N. Commission on Transnational Corporations, Sixth Session, Mexico City, June 23–July 4, 1980, *Progress Made Towards the Establishment of the New International Economic Order: The Role of Transnational Corporations,* Report of the Secretariat, May 16, 1980; U.N. Economic and Social Council, *Consumer Protection,* May 14, 1979.

18. See B. Sepulveda (rapporteur), *Work Related to the Formulation of a Code of Conduct,* Commission on Transnational Corporations, October 24, 1980.

19. U.N. Center on Transnational Corporations, *Transnational Corporations in Food and Beverage Processing* (New York: United Nations, 1980).

20. K. Kok Pang, "Value for People: The Potential Role of a Consumer Movement in the Third World," *IFDA Dossier* 18 (July–August 1980).

21. The Haslemere Group, *Who Needs the Drug Companies?*

22. Commission on Transnational Corporations, *Transnational Corporations and the Pharmaceutical Industry: Introduction and Summary of Findings,* April 3, 1979.

23. C. Raghavan, "Technology: Third World Can Cure or Control Diseases with Proper Drug Policies," *IFDA Dossier* 21 (Jan.–Feb. 1981).

24. Oficina de asesores del C. Presidente, *Sistema alimentario mexicano.*

25. UNESCO, *Proyecto de creación de la agencia latino-americana de servicios especiales de informacion—ALASEI* (Paris, 1979).

26. Ibid.

27. Ibid.

28. Nordenstreng K., "Struggle Around New International Information Order" (Finland: University of Tampere, 1979). See also E.G. MANET, "Es Posible un nuevo orden internacional de la informacion?" *Boletin Comisión nacional cubana de la UNESCO* 18, no. 80 (May–June 1979). On the "McBride Report" see UNESCO, *Many Voices, One World: Towards a New, More Just and More Efficient World Information and Communication Order* (Paris, 1980); *Communication in the Eighties: A Reader on the "MacBride Report"* (Rome: IDOC, 1980).

29. J.S.D. Amorim, "O Brasil e o ordem informativa internacional" (Brasilia, July 1980, unpublished paper).

30. See *Conférence intergouvernementale sur les politiques de la communication en Amérique latine et dans la région des Caraïbes, rapport final San José (Costa-Rica) 12–21*

juillet 1976 (Paris: UNESCO); *Conférence intergouvernementale sur les politiques de la communication en Asie et en Océanie, rapport final, Kuala Lumpur (Malaisie) 5–14 février 1979* (Paris: UNESCO).

31. O. Capriles, "From National Communication Policies to the New International Information Order: Some Lessons for Research," (Paper, Twenty-second Assembly and Scientific Conference of the International Association Research [AIERI-IAMCR], Caracas, August 1980).

32. Ibid.

33. F. Fernandez Christlieb, "Diagnóstico sobre los medios de difusión masiva en México y proposiciones para el derecho a la información," *El Dia,* Mexico, July 22, 1980.

34. H. Lottman, "Brazil: A Long Way to Go," *Publishers Weekly,* Nov. 21, 1980.

35. Ibid.

36. *Excelsior,* Mexico, July 18, 1980; E. SAFAR, "Los radiodifusores vs. el Estado," *Revista Ininco,* Caracas, no. 1, 1980.

37. Mattelart and Piemme, *Télévision: enjeux sans frontières.*

38. J. Joüet, "Critique de l'utilisation des médias légers dans le tiers-monde," *Revue Tiers-Monde* 20, no. 79 (July–Sept. 1979).

39. A.K. Biswas, "Sustainable Development," *Mazingira,* 4, no. 1 (1981).

40. See A. Mattelart, "Communications and the Transition to Socialism in Mozambique," in *Mass Media, Ideologies and the Revolutionary Movement.*

41. "TVE: os primeiros passos da televisão nacional," *Tempo,* Maputo (Mozambique), Feb. 8, 1981.

42. Ibid.

43. M. and A. Mattelart, B. Sock, *Projet de communication sociale pour le développement au Mozambique: un essai d'évaluation* (Maputo, Mozambique: Gouvernement de la République populaire du Mozambique and Fonds des Nations-Unies pour L'Enfance [UNICEF], 1980). A first version of this section on the Mozambican experience appeared originally in *Journal of Communication* 32, no. 1 (Spring 1982).

44. P.M. McCarter, "Report on Transborder Data-Flow Policies," *Computer Decisions,* August 1980.

45. J. Sutz, "Reseña de la situación informática de algunos paises de América latina," (Caracas: Cendes-UCV, Nov. 1980, draft).

46. Ibid.

47. O. Gansley, "Loosening the Telecom Link," *Datamation,* Sept. 1980.

48. A. Lloyd, "Sweden Fears DP Reliance," *Datamation,* June 1980.

49. Ibid.

Chapter 5 / Prospects

1. J. Somavia, "Una perspectiva latino-americana: Liberación y autonomía en la década del 80," *IFDA Dossier* 18 (July–August 1980).

2. H. Schiller, "Will Advanced Communicaton Technology Create a New Order," *Media Development,* Journal of the World Association for Christian Communication, London, vol. 27, no. 4, 1980. From the same author, see *Who knows: Information in the Age of the Fortune 500* (Norwood, N.J.: Ablex, 1981).

3. "Building Blocks for Alternative Development Strategies," *IFDA Dossier* 17 (May–June 1980).

4. *Transnationals Information Exchange* (Amsterdam: Transnational Institute, April 1980).

5. Ibid.

6. B. Castleman, "The Export of Hazardous Factories to Developing Nations."

7. J. and F. Caroux, "Le mouvement associatif, critique du système des partis," *Politique aujourd'hui,* Paris, May–June 1980.

8. "Multinationals and Communications," *Multinational Business,* no. 2, 1979, The Economist Intelligence Unit (EIU).

Index